REAL READING,
REAL WRITING

REAL READING, REAL WRITING

Content-Area Strategies

Donna Topping
and
Roberta McManus

Foreword by Richard Vacca

HEINEMANN
Portsmouth, NH

Heinemann
A division of Reed Elsevier Inc.
361 Hanover Street
Portsmouth, NH 03801–3912
www.heinemann.com

Offices and agents throughout the world

The authors and publisher wish to thank those who have generously given permission to reprint borrowed materials:

Lyrics to "One of These Things" are used by permission of the Estate of the late Joe Raposo. Copyright © 1970 by Jonico Music, Inc. Copyright renewed. Rights in the U.S.A. administered by Stage Harbor Publishers Co.

Library of Congress Cataloging-in-Publication Data
Topping, Donna.

Real reading, real writing : content-area strategies / Donna Topping and Roberta McManus ;

    p. cm.
    Includes bibliographical references (p.)
    ISBN 0-325-00428-5 (alk. paper)
    1. Content area reading. I. McManus, Roberta. II. Title.

LB1050.455 .T68 2002
428.4'07'1—dc21   2001059365

Editor: Robin Najar
Production editor: Sonja S. Chapman
Cover design: Joni Doherty
Typesetter: House of Equations, Inc.
Manufacturing: Steve Bernier

Printed in the United States of America on acid-free paper

06   05   04   03   VP   3   4   5

To our families, with love and thanks

CONTENTS

FOREWORD

Every once in awhile a book comes along with a winning combination—one that has great content, a strong voice, and a collaborative partnership between authors. This book is such a book. Donna Topping and Roberta McManus share themselves—their professional life experience—as much as they do a set of compelling instructional strategies for helping students learn with science texts. Topping, a university-based literacy educator, and McManus, a middle school science educator, team up to produce one of the most readable and sensible texts for connecting literacy and learning that I have come across in a long time.

This is a real book for real teachers. Someone once said that nothing is as practical as a good theory. Yet I wager that Topping and McManus would argue that there is nothing as theoretical as a good practice. And this is what they share with you. These authors won't put you to sleep with long theoretical forays into text-based learning. Nor will they patronize you with cookie-cutter solutions to practical problems that teachers face daily with alliterate learners (those students who can read, but choose not to use reading to learn) and struggling readers (those students who continually find it difficult to comprehend what they read). Instead, Topping and McManus will take you on a journey—their journey as teachers—and share with you the lessons they learned as they grappled with problems and issues related to content literacy—the ability to use reading and writing to learn with text. As they put it in the opening lines of this book, "We like theory, but we love what works in practice."

Upon reading the manuscript of this book, I immediately characterized it as a "third wave" textbook on content literacy. In 1970, my mentor, Hal Herber, wrote the first definitive textbook on reading in the content areas. Hal's book represented the "first wave" of textbooks devoted exclusively to subject matter learning through reading. Herber believed that content-area reading can make a difference in the school lives of young adolescents and teenagers. He contended that "content determines process." Science content, for example, determines the approach that science teachers would take as they show students how to use reading to learn subject matter. Rather than teach reading skills apart from the subject matter, Herber argued that it was content teachers' responsibility to show students how to adapt skills to the demands of the content in their disciplines.

Although several "reading in content area" books followed Herber's, it wasn't until the 1980s that a "second wave" of textbooks on content literacy (mine included) began to dot the educational landscape. These texts extended the work of Herber and others and piggybacked on the cognitive revolution that occurred in the 1970s and 1980s.

Metacognitive and strategic learning formed an integral part of second wave books on content literacy. These books also recognized that forces within the culture and organization of schools often worked against the use of content literacy practices and exerted enormous influence on the way content area teachers view their roles, think about instruction, and resist the use of content literacy practices. The irony behind such resistance is that content-area teachers genuinely *value* the role that reading and writing plays in learning, but often fail to *attend* to reading and writing in their own practices.

As a result, the responsibility for teaching literacy in middle and high schools usually rests with English/language arts teachers and reading specialists—and while they have important roles to play in adolescents' literacy development, English/language arts teachers and reading specialists cannot go it alone. The responsibility for reading and writing is a shared one, belonging to all teachers in all subjects. All too often, however, teachers misinterpret content literacy as meaning, "Every teacher is a teacher of reading." This slogan is one of those unfortunate utterances that does more damage than good. Even today, more than thirty years after Herber's seminal textbook was published, there is considerable evidence to indicate that content literacy practices do not easily find their way into subject matter classrooms in middle and high schools, despite the attention given it by literacy researchers and educators. And this is where a "third wave" of books on content literacy can make a valuable contribution to teaching and learning in content areas such as science.

Third wave books, such as the one you are about to read, are written by teachers for teachers. Topping and McManus believe every teacher is a teacher. Period. End of story. To the extent that texts play a role in academic learning, a content teacher needs to consider instructional strategies that will help students learn with texts without sacrificing attention to content. The authors of this book share what works for them based on their own journey as teachers. Who could ask for more?

—Richard T. Vacca
Kent State University

ACKNOWLEDGMENTS

We must begin by thanking those who were with us when we began this collaborative journey of weaving literacy into the content area. Morton Botel, author of the maverick and way-ahead-of-its-time *Pennsylvania Comprehensive Reading/Communication Arts Plan (PCRP)* (1977), has influenced our thinking in so many ways with his ever-balanced and realistic blending of theory and practice. Susan Lytle, with Morton Botel, both professors at the University of Pennsylvania, helped us continue to refine our thinking through *The Pennsylvania Framework for Reading, Writing, and Talking Across the Curriculum (PCRP II)*. Marion Dugan, Chuck Gibson, Ken Woodward, Brendan Smith, Carol Birt, and Donna Breylinger, the guides and members of the original Building Leadership Team, were the teachers who were there when it all began.

As we talk to fellow educators, we find that we are not unique in our dedication to what we do. We've listened to other real teachers who speak with the same passion of caring about their students. They have told us that they, too, seek the exchange of ideas and strategies for reaching all learners. Many of our fellow educators have encouraged us to put our ideas in print. We thank them for giving us the impetus to assemble this collection of perspectives, ideas, and activities that have evolved over the years through collaborations in the hallway, in the classroom, over lunch, and on the phone in the evening as we have tried and failed, tried and succeeded in this business of getting all students to learn.

The book is the result of much support from many people. Our colleagues Sandy Hoffman, Ken Woodward, and Doug Bleggi patiently and thoughtfully responded to numerous drafts of this manuscript, offering really great advice and lots of encouragement. Kathryne Hooker painstakingly edited the final draft, noticing things that completely slipped by us in spite of multiple re-readings and Spell-Check, and lovingly brought us food and drink when we were under the crunch of the final deadline. Brad Topping created artwork with mere moments of notice, leaving us wondering why we would ever buy clipart again. Robin Najar, Alan Huisman, and Sonja Chapman from Heinemann were wonderful to work with and provided much help along the way. We're grateful to the colleagues, students, and parents who allowed us to include their thoughts and work and to the educator we met who drew us to the attention of Heinemann.

We must thank the special teachers who share our professional lives every day. Donna's colleagues in the early childhood and elementary education department at Millersville University allowed her a summer *not* to teach so she could get this manuscript complete and never ceased to cheer her on. Roberta's colleagues at the Penn's Grove

Middle School are so much a part of this book and are her second family. All of these people enrich our daily lives.

There would be no grist for this book at all if it hadn't been for our students over the years who have taught us so much—so much more than they'll ever know.

To our families—Brad Topping, Allyson and Ed Stallman, Kathryne Hooker, Mark McManus, Pete McManus, and Rhett McManus—we offer special thanks for enduring our lengthy writing sessions with good humor and always asking, "How's the book?"

Real Reading, Real Writing

CHAPTER 1

REAL JOURNEYS

We're real.

We teach.

We like theory, but we love what works in practice. We don't believe in quick fixes for education and have long since stopped climbing on bandwagons just because they happen to be going by. We're not dewy-eyed novices who are out to save the world, but we're not cynical old hard-liners who are close-minded and counting the years 'til retirement either.

We're real teachers with thirty and twenty-seven years of experience, respectively, in basic and higher education. We spend our days in real classrooms covered with chalk dust and filled with the joys and frustrations that accompany life there. We are professionals who view education as a vocation, not just a paycheck. We are honored to teach and believe that teaching is the most important job in the world.

Our students are real, too. They are as diverse as diverse can be. Many have learned easily; many have struggled. One of our former students is on staff at Harvard Medical School; one is incarcerated for committing cold-blooded murder. One young woman is a TV network newscaster on her way up; another is an unwed welfare mother fighting drug addiction on her way down. Two of our students earned movie roles in a major motion picture; five former students were murder victims in an incident that became the basis for another movie. We've taught students who have gone on to lead responsible lives as doctors, plumbers, mechanics, nurses, teachers, parents, engineers—many of whom give back to their community through volunteer work. Unfortunately, others have taken from their community and served time for drug dealing, grand theft auto, drunk driving, and manslaughter.

Our area and its schools are real, too. The little town that gave us our start in teaching is one in transition, as farmland gives way to the bedroom communities of the suburban East Coast megalopolis. The pastoral charm of rural covered bridges contrasts sharply with the faded beauty of a neglected town center. Tears of pride well up in the eyes of citizens at the town's traditional Memorial Day parade; the same citizens also shed tears of shame when their town became the scene of one of the largest drug busts on the East Coast. The community is highly heterogeneous and is home to CEOs, farmers, laborers, welfare recipients, and white-collar workers. Their views on education are as diverse as they are. Residents range from those who are pro education at any cost to those whose primary concern is that their school taxes never increase to those who appear to have little interest in education at all. We've suffered through an economy that has triggered drastic school budget cuts amid bitter debates and damaged feelings. We call this area home as we deal with education in the real world.

Because we're real, we are put off by treatises for teachers that depict mythical problem-free schools where money is no object, all students learn easily, class size is limited, and the clock never encroaches on planning and teaching time. We are weary of lay editorials that tell us that our schools are failing, because we know of many success stories within our own classrooms. Education is not perfect, but we believe in it and strive on, as you do. This book grows from reality, because we know that you are real, too.

Roberta's Story

I knew that I wanted to teach from the time I was in first grade, and sixteen years later, I was very proud of my new contract that read "SCIENCE teacher for Sixth, Seventh, and Eighth Grades." Note the stress on science. My job was to deliver the content of science. My education to become a teacher had emphasized an inquiry approach to learning, along with a lecture-lab-lecture-lab format. Science was the be-all and end-all. Reading, writing, and talking to facilitate learning were never mentioned.

I still remember my first day in the school district when I was introduced to the two new language arts teachers. As I greeted these colleagues, I wondered which one spoke French and which one spoke Spanish! I was shamefaced when I realized that language arts meant reading, English, and spelling classes. After all, it had been nine years since reading, composition, and spelling had last appeared on a report card of mine. It was a bit of a shock for a secondary-trained teacher to realize that students who were ready to learn about nuclear fission might also find semicolons new and daunting.

What a "dewy-eyed novice" I was! I assumed that the language arts teachers and the math teachers would teach everything there was to know about reading, grammar, writing, the Metric system, graphing, and algebra. I also assumed that their wonderful students would exhibit these well-learned skills in my classroom and we would blaze our way smoothly through the science curriculum. After all, my contract said "SCIENCE teacher." I taught science. I wasn't responsible for those other skills. Needless to say, I quickly became frustrated and so did my students. I assumed too much. My students couldn't, wouldn't, or at least weren't bringing their language arts and math skills into my classroom. They didn't comprehend reading assignments, and I was having to repeat lessons too often. I found myself spoon-feeding information to my pupils because they tuned out lectures and found drawing conclusions in labs very difficult. The way I was teaching wasn't working.

I needed to make some changes. I started to take responsibility for what went on in my classroom. I slowed the pace so that we could discuss expectations for science, math, and language in their essays, reports, and labs. Over the next five years, by trial and error, I stopped assuming and started to teach the process of learning my particular content area. It wasn't easy. I found that not all of my students learned in the same way that I did. (This was before research and information on learning styles was available.) I needed to develop a repertoire of teaching techniques, recognizing that some ideas would work and some wouldn't.

Even though I was respected as a successful teacher, I continued to try to improve my craft. I loved teaching science but knew that something was still missing. Making connections in science was easy for me; therefore, shouldn't I be able to make it easy for every student? I didn't though. Out of 165 students per year, an average of fifteen would fail my course. How could I reach this struggling 9 percent? I wanted immediate answers. To whom could I turn? At graduate school, I continued studying science in courses in which content was still paramount and the process of learning never mentioned. At school I was isolated in my room. Secondary colleagues didn't have the answers I was looking for. But there *were* teachers who taught reading, writing, and science every day—elementary teachers. These were the same people at whom we content majors scoffed because they found watered-down science difficult and read "kiddy lit" books for college credit. Could they possibly have the answers? My annual goals conference with my principal was coming up. Maybe this was my invitation to stretch some more. Not knowing what else to call it, I presented my principal with my first written goal: to "elementarize" my teaching.

Donna's Story

Armed with a B.S. in elementary education, I entered the profession as a first-grade teacher and was immediately overwhelmed with how little I knew about teaching students to read and write. After a year of trial and error, I enrolled in a master's degree program in reading. Through the next four years I refined my understandings of the reading and writing processes while applying that understanding to my teaching. After I received my degree I was offered the districtwide position of language arts coordinator (later to be retitled reading supervisor). My teaching role expanded. Among other duties, I was now the teacher of teachers, providing staff development in reading, writing, and talking not just for teachers of traditional subjects called reading and English, but across the curriculum K–12.

As I worked in and observed middle and high school content-area classes, I was struck by the similarities between my own initial lack of understanding about how students read and write to learn and that of these good and caring teachers. The difference seemed to be that it was assumed that I, the elementary-trained, should know about these things; it was assumed they they, the middle-and-secondary-trained, had no need to know them. Reading and writing were things that students should have learned to do "down there" in the elementary grades or "over there" in English/language arts classes. Content-area classes—social studies, science, math, health—were places in which content was presented; students were on their own as far as the language processes needed to acquire it.

The good and caring teachers I met were frustrated. Their better students responded beautifully to their lectures, passing their tests and writing their papers with flying colors. Others, perhaps most, didn't respond so well. The teachers lectured and made reading assignments, then had to relecture and reread the assignments to the majority of their classes. Many of their students seemed either not to have read at all or to have read with no significant understanding. Why did lecture and assignments work with some and not others?

I paused to reflect on my own secondary education. For the most part, I, too, had sat in classes in which lecture and independent reading and writing assignments were the norm. This had worked for me, hadn't it? I had made it through two college degrees. However, it now occurred to me that perhaps I, like some of these teachers' students, had simply managed to adapt easily to learning through lecture and independent work. I had developed my own systems for reading and writing in the content areas— ones that happened to match my teachers' requirements. What of the others?

It also occurred to me that my colleagues' educational backgrounds were probably like mine. We, having made it into and through college, had developed our own successful systems for learning without having been taught how. As a result, was it possible that we simply taught the way we were taught, assuming that this would work for all as it had for us? Was there something more that we should be doing?

I was disturbed when I heard explanations like, *They* (meaning elementary and language arts teachers) just aren't teaching kids how to read and write anymore. Coming from the elementary school, I knew this was not true. Students in our district received a strong base in reading and writing in the elementary grades. Under the tutelage of the same elementary teachers who taught them to read and write, these students applied that reading and writing to learning in science, math, social studies, and health. What happened, then, when they reached the secondary content-area classrooms? Why didn't they apply what they had done so successfully before? The issue of "transfer," of being able to apply reading and writing to more sophisticated learning environments, raised its head.

Collaborating to Find Answers

We came via separate journeys to a shared "felt need." One called it the need to "elementarize," the other called it "transfer," but the conclusion was the same: we needed to do more to help all students learn, not just the ones who learned easily or in the same way we had. The serendipity of a grant-funded project, Project CARES (Communication Arts and Educational Services), brought us together for the first time. Our district was asked to participate in a countywide pilot of the new statewide plan, *The Pennsylvania Comprehensive Reading/Communication Arts Plan (PCRP)* (Botel 1977). Our intermediate school (grades 6–8) was chosen as the pilot school. While most districts chose to concentrate on their elementary schools or secondary English departments, we created a team of teachers (to become known as the Building Leadership Team, or BLT) from the content areas. Thus, the two of us set out with principal Ken, social science teacher Brendan, language arts teacher Carol, and reading specialist (another) Donna to explore the infusion of reading and writing into content-area instruction at the secondary level.

As grant-funded projects are wont to do, CARES ended, the BLT disbanded, but collaboration between the two of us has continued. Twenty-three years have ensued since our first conversation in the storeroom-cum-faculty-meeting-room. (Ah! The working conditions of real teachers!) Donna went on to earn her Ph.D. and is now a university professor who teaches teachers. Roberta continues to teach middle school science, serve as a consultant to school districts, and stay involved in various projects that keep her excited about teaching. Time and distance, however, have not dulled an important lesson we learned from our early work together; that is, real teachers need one another. Before the term was coined and popularized, we found that reflective practice, the deliberate and ongoing thought and talk about our work (not just the cathartic whining and complaining we all do in the faculty room), is central to our survival as a profession. Both of us continue to take ownership for our teaching by researching our own practices and sharing questions and insights about what we do.

Neither of us claims to have a corner on what the other knows, nor the time and opportunity to do what the other does; together, however, we are stronger at what we do because of our collaboration. When Roberta teaches her middle school students, she knows that her pedagogy is strong because she has had Donna to anchor it in learning theory. When Donna espouses theory to her teachers-to-be, she knows that she has had Roberta to anchor it in practice that works.

So, real teachers, this book is for you. It is not a heady tome of theory, but it is heavily influenced by theory. It is not a copymaster "how-to" book, but it is filled with practical stories of classroom practices that work. Every teaching strategy you find here is one we have used with real students. We have watched their grades improve and asked them which strategies helped them learn. We share these ideas with you because we hope that with a little tweaking to adapt them to your content area, they will help you in your journey as real teachers.

Bon voyage!

CHAPTER 2

REAL SITUATIONS, REAL TIMES, REAL PLACES

Schools exist within their cultures and times. To act as if we teach in a vacuum, un-affected by the rest of society, is shortsighted. To present this book as a collection of ideas and strategies that, by itself, will cure education's ills is equally shortsighted. So some reflections on society at large, and on the educational communities in which we work, provide the context into which to fit our ideas and activities.

The Last Half of the Twentieth Century Revisited

Many of us remember the public outcry about the condition of literacy uttered by the American conscience in the 1950s (Flesch 1955, Ravitch 1983). Headlines at the corner newsstands alerted us that Johnny could no longer read very well, college freshmen were finding it difficult to write a simple English sentence, and SAT scores were tumbling. This only compounded the national embarrassment Americans felt after losing the space race to the Soviets with their 1957 Sputnik launch. The finger of blame, of course, pointed directly at the schools. We were failing to teach. American education was duly chastised. Not only were we failing to prepare a nation technologically, but literacy now seemed to be eluding us as well.

Education reacted in various ways (Ravitch 1983, Goodlad 1984, Gibboney 1994, Tyack and Cuban 1995). Experiments were added to science curricula. "New math" was born. Enormous amounts of federal money poured into literacy education to fund quick-fix instruction. Regardless of the name, the underlying premise seemed to be: if Johnny couldn't read, write, and take his tests, then scientifically and systematically we would see that he could. Reading and writing were broken down into a minutia of subskills ranked from the simplest to the most complex. Johnny was to be taught these in order, with the certainty that he would, at the conclusion, put them all together and read and write.

He didn't. With the passage of time, not only was he not reading, writing, and taking his tests better, he appeared to be doing these things a bit less successfully. Looking back at this phenomenon from a societal perspective, it seems that when Johnny was suddenly rendered less literate, it was not so much that the schools had changed, but that the society in which Johnny lived was changing. Fader and McNeil, early advocates of literacy, spoke to this in *Hooked on Books*:

> Of the public events which have had the most profound influence upon American education since the end of the Second World War, a chronological ordering might begin with the GI Bill, the advent of the Television Era, and the 1954 Supreme Court decision which began desegregation of Southern schools, continue through Sputnik, the war in Vietnam, and the revolution exported from Berkeley, then conclude with the movement for women's liberation and the use of busing to begin desegregation of Northern schools. These eight events, seen in a lengthening perspective, now seem to me to fall into two distinct categories. Standing by itself, enormous and uncomprehended in its implication, is the advent of the Television Era. Standing together, the remaining seven form a second group educationally less significant in its entirety than the single, pandemic fact of television. (1968, 22)

TV, the Great Cultural Transmitter

Real teachers, we know you are concerned about the influence of television. Concerns about television exist on three levels. The first is the most obvious, having been the subject of a number of writers for a number of years (Trelease 1995, Winn 1985 and 1987, Postman 1985). Simply put, our students watch it too long and too late, most often in the earliest and most impressionable years of life. Television viewing is second only to sleeping as an occupier of time; students spend more hours in front of the TV than in the classroom. Students watch shows that often are inappropriate, a situation exacerbated by the availability of cable TV movie channels and video rentals. By the time our students graduate from high school, they will have witnessed eighteen thousand violent crimes and have seen countless commercials in which they are one-sidedly pitched to with no recourse to truth in advertising. What does this do to their ability to be sensitive to the human condition and their ability to be critical consumers?

Our second level of concern is a bit more hidden: what is it they are *not* doing while they are watching all this TV? Television viewing is a passive act that requires nothing of the viewer, hence its hypnotic appeal midst hectic lifestyles. It truly is the great mental neutral. When watching TV, our students are not necessarily required to think. They are not engaged in conversation, nor are they reading or writing. Donna has a sign in her kitchen that reads, "Whatever happened to Parcheesi?"—our students are not playing games that require thinking and strategizing either. Our physical education colleagues tell us that TV's effects are not limited to cognition. They see the lethargy and lack of physical fitness that come from the "couch potato syndrome" in their classes as well. This second level of concern raises some real questions about the compatibility of our students' primary wake-time activity with what we espouse for them in school. The two seem quite antithetical.

And if the first two levels of concern are not frightening enough, the third is the most insidious and, we believe, the most dangerous. Not only are our students not reading, writing, thinking, and conversing—the things that are the bastions of school—*they are not seeing anyone else do them either*. How do our young people assimilate the values of their families and their society—by what we adults *say* or *do*? There is a tremendous amount of lip service paid to literacy. It is an issue like apple pie, Mom, and world peace, even championed by first ladies like Barbara and then Laura Bush. One would be hard-pressed to find people who would argue against literacy, but by precept and example, what do we as a society model for our youth?

To bring this into focus a bit better, here are three things you can try in your own community. First, go into a typical American home in which your students find themselves—their own homes, those of their grandparents, babysitter, friends, or the people next door. Walk into the main living space, the room in which this family seems to spend its time—the kitchen, the great room, the family room, the TV room. (Isn't it telling that we used to have rooms called libraries, while we now have TV rooms?) What appears to be valued in this family? Do you see books, newspapers, magazines, paper and pencils—the very tools of literate people? Or do you see a pronounced absence of these artifacts and, instead, a large screen TV, VCR, videotape rack, and video games?

Second, listen to conversations that occur when people get together casually (and even in the faculty room!). What are people saying about what they did last night? Are they discussing a great book they read, a thought-provoking article in a magazine or newspaper, or the latest episode of a sitcom or this week's made-for-TV movie?

The third thing requires a bit of effort and courage. Call (or better yet, go to) your local library and ask for the average monthly circulation. Next, call your local video rental store, or in many towns *stores*, and ask the same question. We did this several years ago and the results staggered us. The average monthly circulation of the public library in our very small town was four thousand books, while the circulation of the video stores was twenty thousand videos.

The Lack of Predisposition Toward Literacy

Add to TV the video explosion, the Internet, and other societal changes within the last half of the twentieth century. Consider the rise of dual-career families, single-parent families, families in turmoil, families with drug and alcohol problems, families dealing

with abuse, poverty, and homelessness. The image of a nuclear family in which children gather nightly at their father's knee to hear a good story and absorb the values of
literacy certainly seems to exist only in a Norman Rockwell painting.

Let's go back to when Johnny's reading was found wanting. What did we do? Something very akin to this: Assume a group of nine children has never seen or heard of baseball and you say to them, "I'm going to teach you to play a game called baseball. Line
up over here and let's have batting practice. Okay, now move over here and let's have
catching practice—now sliding practice—now pitching practice. Very good. Now—*play
baseball!*" It doesn't take a Sammy Sosa to tell you this won't work. Even though these
young people have practiced the specific subskills of the game, they have no idea what
the game itself is all about.

When Johnny began to "lose" his literacy, education responded by attempting to
teach him the specific skills and drills of the game when he didn't even know what the
game involved or why it was important. He (and millions of other Johnnys and Judys
since) was being raised in a society that was no longer predisposing its youth toward
literacy. This does not mean he was being predisposed *against* literacy; no one was saying that reading and writing were not important. What Johnny was hearing, however,
was, "your teachers will take care of that." Johnny's society was not modeling the value
of reading and writing, either by precept or example.

Real teachers must teach within the context of the society that surrounds the real
students they teach, a society they often feel powerless to control (Welsh 1986; Friere
1985,1989; Apple 1996; Routman 1996; Gibboney and Webb 1998, Taylor 1998, Coles
2000, Kohn 2000, among others). Sometimes, however, the school system or school
unit in which they teach seems to be outside their control as well.

An Ever-Changing Spectrum of Initiatives From Within

Real teachers know that the emergence of the latest guru, changes in administration,
and the need to fill up inservice days create an ever-changing spectrum of initiatives
with which to cope, leading us to ask, Do we know where we're going in education?
Our colleague Maryanne quipped one day about education's "new idea du jour." A quick
three-minute brainstorming of initiatives that had come our way in the last decade
yielded this list:

adolescent behavior	middle school concept
attention deficit disorder	mission statement
attention deficit-hyperactive disorder	multicultural education
AIDS awareness	multiple intelligences
benchmarks	new teacher induction
brain research	oppositional defiance disorder

career awareness

cooperative learning

coteaching

curriculum scope and sequence

direct instruction

diversity

effective discipline

every student a gifted student

Four Blocks

gender bias

hate groups

Here's Looking at You 2000

high school accreditation

higher-order thinking skills

inclusion

individualized educational plans

instructional support teams

interdisciplinary curriculum approach

Internet protocols

learning styles

lesson design

mainstreaming the special-education
    student

meeting the needs of learning-
    disabled students

mentoring programs

outcomes-based education

planned course format (required by our state)

professional development plan

safe schools

school-to-work

self-esteem

sexual harassment

small learning communities

standards

state testing

student assistance team

student at-risk program

suicide prevention

Teacher Expectations and Student Achievement

team teaching

technology in the classroom

textbook selections studies

time on task, engaged time, and allocated
    learning time

twelve goals of quality education (for our state)

violence in schools

whole language

writing across the curriculum

writing process

. . . and by the way, don't forget that real
    teachers take time to teach.

You can probably add to this list from your own experiences! Initiatives seem to come, go, and be recycled under new names within short periods of time in our profession. We certainly would not question the value of any of these or the knowledge and sincerity of those who developed them. However, swallowed whole, they appear little more than a jumble of jargon aimed at frustrating the conscientious, jading the cynical, or both.

Educational movements seem to burst onto the scene like fireworks, eagerly greeted with enthusiasm yet burning only briefly before disappearing into the night sky (Ravitch 1983, Gibboney 1994, Tyack and Cuban 1995). Why do these initiatives fail to be cure-alls for education's ills? Why does nothing seem to stay with us? Why do things touted with such great promise so often fail to deliver over the long term?

We strongly suspect the transient nature of educational innovations may be the simple result of teachers', administrators', or whole school systems' not knowing where they are going and then, not surprisingly, wondering why they are not getting anywhere: witness the annual ritual of goal setting in many districts. If educators do not have a base of beliefs, a platform from which to operate, they are fated forever to jump from bandwagon to bandwagon, hoping that something will deliver on its promise to cure all ills.

So, What's a Real Teacher to Do?

Reduced federal and state aid—revolt of taxpayer groups—decline of the nuclear family—increases in homelessness, domestic violence, substance abuse, and dropout rates—curriculum initiatives arriving at whirlwind pace: real teachers do teach within situations, times, and places that can seem overwhelming. We also know that real teachers go on, motivated by their commitment to the students they teach. We have experienced the same frustrations. Rather than being reduced to jadedness or cynicism, we have reflected deeply about our belief system in order to identify the glue that holds our commitment to teaching together.

CHAPTER 3

REAL DESTINATIONS

If we know where we're going, we just might get there; if we don't, we shouldn't be all that surprised when we don't arrive. We've experienced the woes of real teachers. It's easy to become overwhelmed, to burn out, and to assign blame. Rather than succumb to the pressures from without and within, however, we have chosen to remain committed to this business of teaching. What has helped the most has been our ongoing reflection on our craft: finding out where we stand, where we think we're going, and how we think we're going to get there.

Several years ago, Donna and her family went on a cross-country trip. This trip was predicated on the convergence of two key factors: the itinerary and the vehicle. The itinerary—where to go, what to see, and how long to stay—was central; otherwise they would have roamed around aimlessly for thirty-five days only to return home and wonder what they accomplished, what they could have seen if they had planned better. The vehicle that would convey them (plane? train? car? van?) was just as important. Without that vehicle, the wonderfully planned itinerary would have been a paper exercise only, a fantasy to imagine from the living room armchair.

We take our students on a thirteen-year journey called school. We, too, have an itinerary. It's called the curriculum and it tells us where to go, what to see, and how long to stay there. While school would be sorely ineffective without its "itinerary," it requires a "vehicle" to convey it to our students. Just as Donna's cross-country trip required a van to keep it from being merely an armchair fantasy, curriculum requires the use of vehicles—the communication processes of reading, listening, viewing, writing, and speaking—to convey its power to our students. This notion of itinerary (content) and vehicle (processes) strongly undergirds all that we do in our classrooms.

Responding to the Students
We Take on These Trips

We can no longer assume that the Johnnys and Judys who come to us fully understand the "games" we want them to play. Therefore, we can no longer mete out only the subparts of the whole processes of reading, writing, listening, and speaking in any of our subjects, assuming that the students have in place the necessary skills and strategies for reading and writing in science, history, math, or health. We must not just tell but *show* our students what it is we want them to do, how we—the mature adults— read and write in our specific content areas, and how we strategically control ideas and information within them. It's easy for educators to resent having to do this, and to argue, that's not my job—I shouldn't have to—everyone else has abdicated. We understand this frustration. However, the job of real teachers is to *teach*, to do whatever is needed to get real students to learn. Our schools must reflect their culture and times, and we must change accordingly.

The "Teacher" aka the "Coach": Process, Modeling, and Strategies

Coaches who teach have always been given a bad rap—sometimes deserved, sometimes not. However, coaches on their fields of play understand what it takes to get kids to learn. They believe that all kids can play their sport. They don't cancel the season if they lack good players. Coaches teach them all, no matter what their abilities, building on what's there. They deserve our respect and scrutiny. We have much to learn from them.

Every autumn since the age of ten, Roberta has played, coached, or refereed field hockey. She has observed many coaches as they structure their practices around three basic tenets, which we now include in our belief system for teaching:

- Involve students in the *process* of the game.
- *Model* how to do what the game requires.
- Present *strategies* for playing the game successfully under a variety of conditions and variables.

They call it coaching; we call it teaching.

Would a basketball coach ever conduct his entire practice standing behind a podium, lecturing a new junior varsity team ("Set a pick at the top of the key and roll off with a layup on the left through the low post position. Go do it, and I'll assess it on Friday at our first game")? Certainly not. Coaches know that court time is important. Players need time to scrimmage, to play the game, to engage in the *process* of the sport in order to establish the proper context for the specific skills and drills. Coaches also know that verbal explanations are not enough. Our real basketball coach comes out from behind that lectern, moving among the players, feinting, dribbling, shooting, and scoring. In other words, he *models* the behavior desired so that the novices can see how an accomplished player does it. Of course, our coach follows the explanation and modeling with *strategic* information ("If they block the low post position. . . . The player setting the pick then needs to. . . .").

Why are we so willing to teach when we coach but so unwilling to coach when we teach? Coaching *is* good teaching. Why should the reverse not be true? We should regularly engage students in the real *processes* of reading and writing for as authentic a set of purposes as possible in real schools; we need to engage them in playing the whole game. Then we should *model*, "think aloud" for them, everything we ask them to do—showing them how we read a math text differently from a novel, and write an essay in history differently from a personal narrative in English, how a scientist deals with information on a lab report, or how studying theorems in geometry is different from studying body systems in health. Finally, we need to guide our students in developing a repertoire of *strategies* for reading, writing, studying, and retrieving information presented to them in a wide variety of contexts.

It's ironic that all the above probably strikes most of us, initially, as cheating. What? Show them how we read, write, and think? We have been led, perhaps by how we were taught, to think that the only valid form of teaching is questioning: I (the teacher) ask you (the students) the question. In that act of questioning, we tell ourselves that we are teaching. But is that stance a teaching posture or a testing posture? Much of our subconscious definition of teaching really has been a definition of testing: we tell our students to read, listen, or view information, then we ask them to answer questions about it without ever equipping them with a model and set of strategies for doing so.

It's also ironic that when all else fails, when there truly seems to be nothing left, *we'll teach*. For example: Ms. A's students have just read a portion of a text and she poses a question about it. She asks a sampling of students for the answer, and when it is not forthcoming, she calls on José in the front row. José is her "ace in the hole." He sits up front so he can hang on her every word, comes from a wonderful home, is as bright as can be, and always knows the answer. Today, however, even José seems confused. With her blood pressure rising and veins bulging in her neck, Ms. A says in a high-pitched voice, "Don't you see? Look at the way the author has organized the text. The heading of this section lets you know that the main idea is so-and-so. The sidenote tells you the same thing, and the author restates it in the last sentence of the last paragraph!" Then, in abject frustration, she heads for the faculty room not to collaborate and share ideas but to vent. When worse came to worse, what did she do? *She taught*. She taught the *processes* of learning. What would have happened if she had facilitated that learning in the beginning by showing her students how the whole text was organized, if she had modeled how a mature reader would go about reading it, if, like the coach, she had not left the notions of process, modeling, and strategies to chance but had incorporated them into the very being of her teaching?

Is it cheating for real teachers to teach? Ask a coach. They know how to get kids to learn. Maybe the rest of us assume too much.

Stamp Out Assumptive Teaching

You know how this works. The graduate schools blame the undergraduate schools for students' ill preparation. In turn, the undergraduate schools blame the high schools, who blame the middle schools, who blame the elementary schools, who blame the pre- schools, who blame the parents, who blame it all on the defective genes of their spouse. An exaggeration? We don't think so. We've sat in conferences and heard many a parent say, Well, my husband/wife never was too good at math/science/reading either. Haven't you?

We like to lay blame within our ranks as well. Students have difficulty writing a history essay? The history teacher blames the English teacher. They can't set up an equa- tion? The science teacher blames the math teacher. We lament, If only *everyone else* were doing her job, *I* could get my students to learn my content. Humans seem to have the unendearing tendency to size up a bad situation and then find someone else to be at fault. It's so much more comfortable to brand someone else as the culprit than to look inside and see what we could be doing to make the situation better. When we assign blame, we expend a great deal of energy on things that are not only nonproductive but counterproductive.

When we, as teachers, point the finger elsewhere, we set up a pattern of what Harold Herber (1970) long ago called "assumptive teaching." In assumptive teaching everyone assumes that it was *someone else's* job to teach students the skills and strate- gies they need to be successful learners. Consequently, *no one* teaches them. Farfetched? Consider two assignments commonly given in content-area classrooms: study for Friday's test, and read Chapter 2 for tomorrow. Embedded in both directives is the assumption that *someone else* taught them how to study geographical data or read economic reports and how doing so is different from studying for math or reading literature.

Roberta recalls doing this in eighth-grade science, but this is not a characteristic of the middle and secondary levels alone. Donna remembers all too well saying to her beginning-of-the-year first graders, "Open your books to page twenty-three," only to find some little ones leafing through the back of the book, some searching the front of the book, and some holding their books upside down. Her reaction? "Well, what in the world do we pay those kindergarten teachers for? You'd think that with all I have to teach about reading and writing, they could at least teach kids how to find a page in the book!" Assumptive teaching is everywhere.

How do we make certain that our students acquire the skills and strategies they need to function successfully not only in our classes but in life? To avoid assumptive teaching, we need to share accountability across all grades and subjects, being deliber- ate about showing and telling students how to do the things we ask them to do within the particular contexts of the subjects we teach. To break the assumptive teaching mold, we need to remember that teaching and learning exist on a continuum, as we lead our students from dependence on us to independence from us. In one sense, this is a way of conceptualizing our overall school program, seeing kindergarten as dependence and twelfth grade as independence. More specifically, we can apply this concept to every grade, every unit, and every lesson. If we regard the beginning of any time period— the year, a unit, a lesson—as dependence and then deliberately model for students the behavior we want them to practice, we can gradually release control to them, have them function more independently as time goes by.

Herber (1970) countered the that's-not-my-job argument like this:

> Teachers may feel that there is too much "hand-holding". . . . In a sense good teaching *is* hand-holding; it is literally leading the pupils through a process until such time as they can walk alone. Rarely does that time come abruptly. . . . With respect to any skill, independence is an ultimate state not an immediate one. (30)

If every teacher in every grade and subject shared the accountability to teach this way, wouldn't we have less assumption and more competence? It sounds so simple, and yet we practice the opposite. We assume that someone else held their hands, so we give only a few directions and expect them to walk alone. We must stop teaching assumptively and take responsibility for *all* the learning in our classrooms. We must teach not only the content but also (and more important) the processes of learning. We must provide our students with a repertoire of strategies that they can use to acquire knowledge throughout their lifetime.

Preparing Students for Real Life: Critical Questions to Guide Our Teaching

The task of preparing our students for real life is an overwhelming charge. We can easily become preoccupied with today—getting them to learn the difference between fission and fusion, or the events leading to World War II—and fail to remember that our superordinate goal is to make sure that they go out into the world as fully functioning citizens. As John Dewey (1916) told us long ago, that's the ultimate destination.

We spend a lot of time in education running around wildly looking for *answers* (will cooperative learning do the trick? will a better mission statement assure adequate preparation?) when perhaps our real problem is that we don't know what our *questions* are. We reiterate our earlier point: if we don't know where we're going, we increase our likelihood of not getting there. Likewise, if we don't know what *questions* are important to guide our search, we probably will not find the *answers* we're looking for.

Over the years, we have come to a commonsense assertion about our teaching: our job is to make sure our students develop a repertoire of strategies for reading, listening to, and viewing all kinds of information that is presented to them; for composing through writing and speaking; and for knowing how to learn for a lifetime. Is there one among us, first-grade teacher or graduate school professor, who would not agree that these experiences are critical to learning at any age in any subject? As we will see in Chapter 11, employers agree. If we accept these as essential life preparation experiences, our questions for education become:

- Are we guiding our students to know how to *read, listen to, and view* information that is presented to them?
- Are we guiding our students to *write and speak* appropriately for the tasks at hand?
- Are we guiding our students to *know how to learn for a lifetime*?

Against this backdrop of critical questions, all the "new ideas du jour" have value *only if* they provide potential answers to these questions. Should we get involved with new movement X or buy program Y? Gee, I don't know. Will it help our students read, listen, and view more effectively? Will it help them write and speak more effectively? Will it develop their ability to learn? If so, it deserves our attention; if not, why should we bother?

Imagine a K–12 school system in which every teacher in every subject made a conscious point of reinforcing these commonsense assertions in the daily life and lessons of their classrooms. Would we not send citizens out into the world fully prepared for lifelong learning? We are fooling ourselves if we think learning ends with high school graduation. In this busy, technopaced world we constantly are having to absorb and adjust to new information. We have to learn how to program VCRs, understand computerese, slog through tax forms, write résumés, reach consensus in the workplace, understand medical information, and on and on. It is our professional responsibility to make sure that our students learn not only the content of our courses but also how to use reading, writing, and language to assimilate new information, both as students and adults.

These essential questions are central in our vision of where we're going. How will we get there? By remembering what the coach knows: engage students in the real processes, model what we want them to do, and develop a repertoire of strategies for using language to learn. Above all, we must share accountability with our colleagues and avoid assuming that it's *someone else's job*.

The Trip Starts Slowly

Oh, the impatience we feel as real teachers! Roberta circles December 13 on her calendar each year. Until that date, the trip she is taking in her science room is a very slow one. It takes time to guide her students through the processes and strategies, modeling carefully as she goes along. At times it seems as though she will not be able to "cover" all of her curriculum. However, an interesting thing always happens. By mid-December the pace picks up rapidly. Empowered by control over their own learning, her students begin to internalize these processes to the point that they are able to absorb content very quickly. The vehicle is up and running at full speed, and the sites fly by enroute toward the final destination.

Paul's trip through school had had its share of detours and bumps in the road. Around the middle of December he approached Roberta's desk with a reading guide that he had completed in connection with a magazine article she had assigned. He said, "Boy, Mrs. McManus, this was tough." She said, "Yes, but look at what time it is." He replied, "Eleven-twenty—so what?" Then it dawned on him that he had completed the reading successfully in only half a period. He was thrilled. "Look at me now! That would have taken me two periods in the beginning of the year!"

The time spent on process seems tedious in the beginning of the year, but the payoff is great. During the first meetings of the Building Leadership Team, Roberta fretted over the content she would have to forego in order to teach the processes of learning. At one meeting she pointedly asked Donna and Principal Ken, "So, which of my units will you authorize me to omit so that I can teach them how to learn?" Filled with uncertainty themselves, they mumbled a sort of nonanswer about "seeing how it goes." Omitting a unit never became an issue. Because Roberta's students learned how to learn, slow though it was in the beginning, they not only flew through her standard units, she was able to add more!

Let's Control What We Can

So much seems so out of our control in education. The broader structures of society and the infrastructures of school districts and schools are what they are. Decisions about such things as curriculum, standards, and state assessments often march on in spite of our opinions. Still, we teach all those who come through our door, turning no one away. We teach those who want to—and can—learn easily, as well as those who don't want to and can't. Our jobs are tough. But real teachers know that what goes on in our rooms when the door is closed—*how we teach*—is firmly *within* our control. The decisions we make about what to do and how to do it make all the difference in the world for students. Rather than fixating on what we can't control, we need to take action on what we can. With this in mind, the words of St. Francis of Assisi ring true: "Grant us the wisdom to know the difference."

CHAPTER 4

READING: CONVEYING THE BIG PICTURE

Real teachers are well acquainted with frustration. They see it on the faces of students who have difficulty comprehending their reading assignments, are unable to follow written directions, need lessons repeated, or want to be spoon-fed answers to tests and assignments. Teachers feel their own frustration when students arrive in September with extremely negative attitudes toward reading textbooks.

The blame for this frustration is placed on many shoulders. We accuse textbook companies of presenting material too briefly—can World War II *really* be explained in three pages, or photosynthesis in two paragraphs? Parents unwittingly contribute to this negativity when they beg off helping with homework by saying, *I can't help you with that—I don't understand it—I never had that in school.* The subliminal message is *Reading is hard; your adult parent can't do it.* And sometimes we contribute to the negativity ourselves when we say things like, *Didn't you learn how to read in English/reading/any-other-class-than-mine?* No wonder so many students approach their reading assignments as something to finish rather than as a means to gain new knowledge.

We love it when we say, read Chapter 2 for tomorrow, listen to today's lecture, or watch this video, and students *do it* period and especially when they do it with such understanding that we can get on with our business of lecturing, clarifying, and stretching them to the max. What happens, though, when our commands to read, listen, or view go unheeded or are met with difficulty? Research in comprehension underscores time and again that learning is not a passive act, akin to having knowledge poured into an empty vessel (Anderson and Armbruster 1984; Anderson et al. 1985; Goodman 1984; Pearson et al. 1978; Pearson and Fielding 1991; Smith 1994). Successful readers actively construct meaning when they read, listen, and view.

Actively Engaging Students

Think about students in your classes. Make two lists. On one, list the students who just seem to "get it" when they read your texts, listen to your lectures, or view your videos. On the other, list those who don't. You may not know why, or what the ones who "get it" are doing that the ones who don't "get it" aren't, you just know there is a difference.

Now look at Figure 4–1. Do you recognize anyone here? Our successful and unsuccessful readers differ in their overall level of activity and involvement in the act of making meaning from texts. Our good readers recognize that reading is making meaning. They *access their prior knowledge*. They think of what they already know and build bridges from this to the new information they are about to encounter. They *hypothesize and predict*, combining what they already know with their best guesses about what the new information will convey. They *visualize*. They make mental pictures of what is happening in the text and of the way the text is organized. They *monitor their comprehension*. They know that the goal of reading, listening, and viewing is meaning and they expect these activities to make sense. When they don't, red flags go up—*This isn't making sense!* Recognizing that it doesn't make sense, they pull from a repertoire of reading strategies to *fix up* the break in meaning.

Our poorer readers, on the other hand, tend to be very passive—dragging their eyes and ears across the page, the teacher's voice, or the screen without actively constructing meaning. Unlike our better readers, they do not make connections with their prior knowledge, hypothesize and predict, or visualize. Since they do not actively associate reading/listening/viewing with making meaning, they don't monitor their comprehension, recognize when something does and doesn't make sense, and employ subsequent fix-up strategies.

Some of our students come to us as active meaning makers. Others don't. The job of real teachers is to structure conditions within our lessons to get *all* students to do

---

GOOD AND POOR COMPREHENDERS

GOOD COMPREHENDERS	POOR COMPREHENDERS
• access prior knowledge	• do not access prior knowledge
• hypothesize and predict	• do not hypothesize and predict
• visualize	• do not visualize
• monitor their comprehension	• do not monitor their comprehension
• use fix-up strategies	• do not use fix-up strategies

Figure 4–1.

what the successful comprehenders do intuitively. The activities in the following chapters *actively* engage students in:

- Using the *processes* of reading, listening, and viewing.
- Seeing a *model* of what these processes look like when they are done well.
- Learning to be *strategic* when using them.

The level of activity they foster increases student involvement. The guidance they provide equips students with the skills and strategies they need to be successful learners.

What Do People Do When They Read?

Let's begin with a very basic question: Do *you* know what you do when you read? Over the years, real teachers have confessed to us (sheepishly, on the sly, and in whispers most of the time) that they really don't know what happens when they read. Roberta notes that no one ever mentioned this in her preservice training as a secondary teacher. Donna, the elementary-trained, felt almost as ill prepared. It is sadly ironic that the very people who are charged with conveying content through texts and who use the processes of reading intuitively so well themselves are the least able to empathetize with those who need to learn how to do them better. Sympathetic, yes (*that poor kid has such difficulty reading—I wish there was something I could do*); empathetic, no. Reading has been on automatic pilot for us for so long that we do it unconsciously, unaware of what really happens when we read. Could this, perhaps, be at the heart of some of our problems in getting our students to do it effectively?

Be honest. Do you know what you do when you read and, therefore, what you ask your students to do every time you say, *Read Chapter 2*? Take a moment to read the following passage, one that Donna intentionally wrote to cause you difficulty, and try to be conscious of what you do when you read.

This task commonly is associated with mammals, genus: human. Their orientation toward the time for completing this task is influenced by how they acquire their subsistence. For some, this task is required anno meridian; for others, post meridian. Educational level appears not to be a factor in influencing this decision; those holding advanced medical degrees and those who fall into the category of unskilled labor alike often can be found performing this task at a time different from the majority of the population.

Regardless of the time, a rather simple sequence seems to exist. First, they must rid themselves of all semblance of that which was used in the preceding time period. Next, they select from an assortment of choices those things that would be deemed most appropriate. (It should be noted that some find that the first two steps are better when reversed; others eliminate step two altogether, having made this decision earlier.)

Before performing the third step, most people elect to engage in an act of purification, this having been recognized as a cultural norm in American society. Having done so, they first add to their persons those items that generally are not shared with the public. The exact choice here depends upon one's gender.

Unless an intermediary step of heat application is needed, the fourth step begins. They place component parts to achieve an overall composite that is appropriate to the anticipated activity and to the image they wish to project. In the vernacular, this often is referred to as achieving "the look."

The final step is quite simple. They look into a full-length reflectoimagographum and check to see if any adjustments are necessary.

Notice that we used a testing posture here. We gave you an assignment with no associated modeling or strategic information. We merely told you to read it. We now ask: *What was that passage about?* We have given this passage to hundreds of very bright elementary and secondary teachers and the responses have ranged from "going to the bathroom" to "going to work" to "getting dressed" to "washing one's hands." Donna constructed this passage based on the activity of getting dressed, but that's not the most important point here. Our second question is the more important one: *How did you figure it out?*

This passage is obviously not an easy read. You had to pull up your repertoire of reading strategies to construct meaning actively. You had to "know about your knowing," that process known as *metacognition* (Palinscar and Brown 1984; Paris et al. 1993). Here are the things that real teachers have told us they did when they tried to make this text make sense. Compare theirs with yours.

I *stopped*, went back, and *reread*.

I *slowed down*.

I thought about *things I do that are like this*.

I tried to *picture it*.

I kept *reading on* to see if something later would make it make sense.

I tried to figure out how it was *organized*. It seemed to be telling me something in sequence (first, next, the final step).

I focused on *key words*—"the look," first, next, final.

I tried to read over a paragraph and then *restate it in my own words*.

I kept trying to *summarize* what I had read before.

I *underlined*.

I jotted *notes* in the margin.

I *talked* to Jennifer—was I allowed to do that?

What the heck is a reflectoimagographum???

Okay, real teachers, what *did* you do with *reflectoimagographum*? Donna made it up, so it's not a word you've encountered in your past reading or vocabulary study.

Chances are, however, you knew it was a mirror. How did you know that? Didn't you use the *context* of the rest of the sentence (look into, full-length, to see), the *phonetic* cues (sounds cued by the letters you saw), and *structural* cues (reflecto = reflects back, *image* = something you see)? Real readers use all those cueing systems when they encounter unknown words.

Our intent in giving this passage to real teachers is to get them to become conscious of strategies so deeply embedded in their successful reading that they are automatic. Our hope is that, in becoming aware of what happens when *they* read, they will be better able to help their students use a broad repertoire of strategies in their reading. These deeply embedded strategies always do come to the surface, but some interesting affective feedback often comes up as well. Here are some of the teachers' remarks:

I felt so dumb!

Why couldn't I understand this? I just knew everyone else was getting this and I wasn't.

When Freda turned the page before I did, I panicked.

I was so glad when I heard Roy turn back to reread this. Maybe he wasn't getting it either.

When you left the room, I real quick asked Kayce what she thought this was about, but I knew this was cheating and I was afraid I'd get caught!

These comments were made by mature, successful readers. Imagine the feelings of our students who find some of the texts we give them as elusive as that getting-dressed passage was for us! Perhaps we assume too often that the texts we give our students in science, history, economics, or math read easily for them because they do for us and that they can successfully be read alone. Perhaps we need to be more empathetic and guide students in acquiring a repertoire of strategies to become more independent—to "get it" on their own. In short, we need to remember to build *scaffolds* between where they are and where they are capable of being, just like a builder does when he is taking a building to its most soaring peak (Bruner 1986; Vygotsky 1962, 1978).

Given that all readers need to be strategic, to be able to cope successfully and confidently with all kinds of texts, what do real teachers do? Could you give the "getting dressed" passage to your students and have them come up with a list of strategies they use when they read? Perhaps. Better yet, give them a difficult passage from your content area. Use it as an opportunity to talk about the different strategies readers use, to model for them how you go about constructing meaning from texts, to elicit their strategies from them, and to develop an action plan for reading texts in your subject. Students read more confidently (*I'm not the only one who has trouble sometimes*) and more successfully when the year begins with a frank discussion on how to go about reading.

Charts like those in Figure 4–2 can highlight reading strategies. Students of all ages love the image of "clicks" and "clunks" (Anderson 1980)—and especially love knowing

WHEN YOU'RE READING...

Ask yourself...

Am I *CLICKING ALONG*? (I get it.)

Have I hit a *CLUNK*? (I don't get it.)

FIX-UP STRATEGIES TO USE WHEN YOU HIT A CLUNK

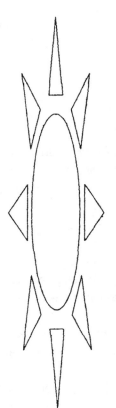

Slow down or stop.
Reread.
Read on.
Connect to something you already know. (Use your prior knowledge.)
Predict or hypothesize.
Make a picture in your head.
Use text aids (pictures, headings, title, graphs).
Figure out the pattern (cause and effect, sequence, listing, comparison/contrast, description, problem-solution).
Identify the controlling idea.
Find key words and signal words (first, second, in summary).
Chunk long, wordy parts into fewer words.
Restate in your own words (paraphrase).
Summarize.
Ask yourself questions.
Ask someone else what they think it says.
Write (underline, jot margin notes, write in your own words).
Use a system to figure out an unknown word:
      Read to the end of the sentence (context).
      Try the first few sounds (phonics).
      Break the word apart (structure).
      Use the dictionary/glossary.
      Ask someone for help.

Figure 4–2. *Action plan for reading*

that their teachers hit clunks when they read, too. Post these charts and refer to them throughout the year. (As an added bonus, you'll have an "instant bulletin board" that never has to be changed!)

Not everyone uses all these strategies all the time, nor is this *the* definitive list. You and your students undoubtedly will have a lot of fun coming up with one that is particularly relevant to the types of texts you read in your class. Starting the year with an ethos that says, *We're a community of readers joining together*, sets a great tone for the rest of the year.

Getting to Know Your Text

"In September all teachers should do an activity to introduce the textbook to their students." We've all heard that line whether in methods classes, inservices, or faculty meetings. Some of us follow through, some don't. Some of us make it a priority; some pay lip service to the idea. Nevertheless, *whatever* the subject or grade level, if a textbook is an integral part of what is taught and tested, we must familiarize students with it.

Many successful readers in middle and high schools have already developed a set of coping skills and apply them to their texts. But what about students who are not so successful? These are the ones who really need our help in making texts make sense. They need to know how to recognize features designed to aid comprehension, examine scope and organization, and discover the strengths and weaknesses of their books. The goal is for them to become competent enough to use their texts independently, noticing how graphs, pictures, and other features are integrated into the main body of the work.

In Appendix A, pages 167–69 is a textbook survey that Roberta uses in her seventh-grade classes. Her students enjoy the confidence of dealing with familiar features such as the table of contents, glossary, and index. The young text examiners are surprised to find some information listed in the table of contents but not the index. (They delight in finding evidence of adult "mistakes.") They stumble and require help with items asking them to look at how chapters are divided. Together, the class and teacher develop a common language for the headings, subheadings, and self-check questions that eases discussions and clarifies assignments throughout the year. They become familiar with special features such as short biographical sketches, career awareness inserts, and information on technology—information that less savvy readers often skip because it's "not the real text." By writing, discussing, and examining the text together, the "two-ton-science book" becomes less intimidating and more user-friendly—a tool ready to become an integral part of the year's learning.

Not all classes rely on regular textbooks. Roberta's eighth-grade physical science classes use primary source material—books, pamphlets, magazines, newspaper articles, and labs. The standard text survey does not work well here. However, even with these materials she remembers that her role is that of teacher-coach. She previews how these materials are organized and presents her game plan for using them.

SQ3R: An Old Friend Revisited

Once Roberta introduces and overviews the course text(s), she has begun to guide her students toward independence. The real task lies ahead—reading and remembering what is in those texts. The teacher-coach recognizes how overwhelming that can be for many students and is prepared to continue showing them how.

One simple way to read and remember is to use the SQ3R study plan. Its mantra of *Survey, Question, Read, Recite, Review* makes reading informational text a less mysterious process. Perhaps you're saying, *But my students don't need this. That's for elementary kids. My students can read the text.* Great! However, what if you want them to read a more sophisticated text? Let's be honest. All literate adults find some writing difficult to follow. Maybe your nemesis is *Scientific American*, the works of John le Carré, or the dreaded tax forms. If you examine your approach to difficult reading, don't you use the steps of SQ3R? Again, we make this same point with our students.

We know some of you are saying, "*Good grief, SQ3R is as old as the hills! I spent money for this book to get new ideas.* SQ3R certainly is not new; its roots go back to the 1930s and it has continued to garner respect since then (Robinson 1961, Anderson and Armbruster 1984; Caverly and Orlando 1991). What is "new" about it is the context in which Roberta uses it. It stops being a cut-and-dried lesson in a reading class and takes on vitality as she models its use in science. Students actively make connections between what they already do as readers and new strategies to try. SQ3R is placed squarely within the community of readers.

Here's what happens. Entering Roberta's classroom on the first day of school, students are greeted with a bulletin board bearing the glow-in-the-dark heading, *The SQ3R Study Plan*. Cartoons with captions outlining the plan invite students' attention. Keep in mind, Roberta teaches *science*. Discussing books and reading in this context is risky, scary, but well worth it. Friendly and frank, she sets the tone for the year: a caring adult is willing to guide you through the process of learning, not just present subject matter to you.

Roberta begins by asking, "How many of you like to read science books for fun?" Only four of her last 472 students have raised their hands. When she asks why not, typical answers are, "It's hard and uses too many big words." Roberta readily agrees and mentions that many science books have sketchy explanations and too-brief summaries. She also points out that new vocabulary is often introduced too rapidly. With further prodding, one brave soul finally admits that reading science is boring. Roberta agrees that it's not thrilling material but promises to provide more interesting reading during the school year.

Students are now ready and willing to hear about a plan to make reading and comprehending easier. Roberta directs their attention to the bulletin board and passes out a form students can use to take notes (Figure 4–3). This ensures that everyone actively engages with each step of the plan as it is explained. Roberta reassures them that they already use SQ3R every time they go to the library or bookstore: they just need to learn to transfer the process to science class.

Here's a typical exchange between Roberta and her students as they participate as a community of readers investigating the use of SQ3R:

ROBERTA: If you don't like to get science books out of the library, what kinds of books do you like? [A discussion of favorite genres ensues, somewhat subdued at first, but more open when students realize that their opinions count.] How do you pick a book out of the library or bookstore? After all, you don't go in and grab the first book that you lay eyes on.

A STUDENT: I look at the cover.

ROBERTA: What do you look for on the cover?

A STUDENT: The title.

ROBERTA: Does it influence your selection? [Students look puzzled.] For example, if the title were something like *Fun and Games for Six-Year-Olds*, would you check it out? [Big chorus of "nos!"] What else do you look for on the cover?

A STUDENT: The picture on the front.

ROBERTA: I'll bet this also influences your decision. I know that if I see an action figure or a baby doll on it, that book's not for me. [Nods and laughter.] What else helps you decide to check out a book?

A STUDENT: The author.

ROBERTA: My favorite authors are Tom Clancy and Dick Francis. What authors do you like? [S. E. Hinton, Judy Blume, and Madeline L' Engel are mentioned every year, but Stephen King is always the most popular author in every class.] How can you read his stuff? You've all got sick minds! I read one of his books and had nightmares for three weeks! [Squeals of delight. Now, everyone has bought into the lesson. The once subdued discussion has become very lively as students interact with their teacher and each other.] What else about a book do you look at before you decide to read it?

A STUDENT: Pictures. Size of print.

ROBERTA: Can you say that you survey a book before you check it out? [Nods from the students.] That's the first step in the SQ3R study plan. When you do this for a library book, you know what to expect from the book. It's the same with science, social studies, or first-aid books. You survey a text, chapter, or section to get a

SQ3R	NOTES	REACTIONS
survey		
question		
read		
recite		
review		

Figure 4–3. *SQ3R listening guide*

general idea of what the reading is about. You look at the layout of your assignments. Are there questions or summaries at the end of the selection? Are subheadings found throughout? Are any pictures, maps, or graphs found in the pages? Surveying takes less than thirty seconds, but it's an important step when you begin a reading assignment. Let's go back to searching for an interesting book in the library. After you've quickly looked at the title, print, author, and pictures, what's your next step?

A STUDENT: I read the back cover or the inside flaps.

ROBERTA: Why?

A STUDENT: To see what it's about.

ROBERTA: In what way?

A STUDENT: Is it fiction or nonfiction?

A STUDENT: What's the genre—historical, horror, romance, mystery, science fiction?

A STUDENT: The setting—past, present, future?

A STUDENT: Does it look interesting to me? Will I want to finish reading it?

A STUDENT: What's the sex of the main character? [Roberta finds that the girls are more comfortable reading a novel where the protagonist is male than vice versa. Why? A topic for another day!]

ROBERTA: This is what questioning is all about. It let's you make predictions about what you will read. It also gives you a purpose for reading. You need to find the answers to your questions in science. We can handle the question part of SQ3R in two ways. One, we can make up questions of our own. If the title of a chapter is "Cells—The Basic Unit of Life," we might ask several questions about that phrase. For example, How small are cells? Can you think of any questions about cells?

A STUDENT: Are all living things made of cells?

A STUDENT: Are all cells alike?

A STUDENT: How many cells are in humans?

A STUDENT: How long do cells live?

A STUDENT: How do cells produce new cells?

ROBERTA: Very good. Next, I want you to be absolutely sure to do this next part of the question phase with every assignment I give you. *Read the questions first!* It drives me absolutely crazy to give kids a worksheet and reading assignment, watch them read everything, then look at the questions, and next start to reread the entire assignment. *Read the questions first!* It doesn't matter if they are the questions in your text or questions on a paper that I've given you. *Read the questions first!* It'll help you concentrate, give you a purpose for the reading, and let you focus on the information that I want you to understand. I see so many kids try to skip this step but, believe me, it makes a big difference. Now we're at the read stage of

SQ3R. We're all readers in this room and know what to do, right? [Yeses and nods of agreement.] What I want you to remember with all of your reading is to read for ideas, not just words. Answer your questions as you go along. I also want you to recognize that reading a science book is different from reading an English anthology or a social studies text. Here, you need to slow down. Read carefully. I'll bet that you do your slowest reading of all in math class. You really need to take in every single word there. I bet you're all thinking, *Okay, I can survey, question, and read library books, but I definitely do not recite or review them!* Well, I think we do. For example, how many of you have ever come to the bottom of a page to realize suddenly that you have no idea what you just read? [All hands go up, including Roberta's.] What do you do?

A STUDENT: Go back and reread.

ROBERTA: Exactly! Do you ever have to do this when you read your school textbooks? [Nods again.] This is called the recite stage. You go over what you've just read to make sure you understood it, can remember it. And if you don't? Go back and read again.

A STUDENT: Reread. Why is it called recite and not reread?

ROBERTA: Would you rather call it reread?

A STUDENT: Yes.

ROBERTA: That's okay with me. Next, we need to apply this recite—or reread—portion of SQ3R to our science reading. How often should you stop and check your understanding? [Discussion follows until students agree that they should stop at the end of each paragraph to monitor their comprehension.] Since you've decided to stop at the end of each paragraph, try to list the main ideas of each paragraph. What should you do if this gives you trouble?

A STUDENT: Reread!

ROBERTA: When you go home tonight, pick up your library book and open to the page at your bookmark. What do you do? [Puzzled frowns.] Don't you have to remember where you are in the story? For example, I'm reading *The Bear and the Dragon,* by Tom Clancy [2000]. When I open the book tonight, I need to remember that trade negotiations between China and the USA have just broken off and the President's men are concerned about the effect on the global economy. If I couldn't remember that, what could I do?

A STUDENT: Reread the last several pages or skim the previous chapter.

ROBERTA: Exactly. I review the story in my mind or review the previous pages to spark my memory. We need to do the same thing in science. At home, you should review the day's work every night. Be sure you understand and are prepared for quizzes and other questions from me. I'll try to start lessons with a quick review also. There. We've just shown how we use SQ3R every time we use library books.

It's automatic, unconscious; we just do it. Now, I want you to do this *consciously* with every reading assignment in science class or social studies or music or whatever.

At this point, Roberta fields questions, checks that her students understand every aspect of SQ3R, and have completed the notes side of their worksheet. Next, she asks students to write their honest reactions to each phase of SQ3R. Circulating around the room, she offers encouragement and gives her reactions to their opinions. Asking students to give their reactions helps them internalize the lesson and understand how they can do what they automatically do with library books with science books as well.

Many students give reactions that teachers always hope to get. For example, Brad wrote the following about *survey*: "Make better grades because you know what you're reading." For *question*, he wrote, "Good idea so you won't have to go back and look for answers." He really understood the lesson and recognized the helpfulness of SQ3R. On the other hand, Amanda said for *survey*, "I've never done before. Sounds stupid." For *read*, "I usually answer the questions when I'm done." She obviously was quite honest and received a great deal of encouragement to try to integrate SQ3R into her approach to reading. (Guess which child found reading easier.) Roberta's favorite reaction page (Figure 4–4) is that of Nick, a man of few words.

Roberta's presentation of SQ3R fills one forty-three-minute period. The class the following day begins with a review of SQ3R and a practical application of it using a science textbook. This first exposure to SQ3R is a whole-class activity, with Roberta modeling the behavior required to move through each phase in order to comprehend the passages being read. Students see that SQ3R not only makes sense but also makes reading easier and increases comprehension.

After these initial presentations, Roberta does not allow SQ3R to be forgotten. She repeatedly reminds students to let the study plan guide their reading. One chemistry exam even contains the question, "What do the letters in SQ3R represent? Pick one letter and explain how it relates to reading science assignments." She urges students to use this study plan and make it an automatic approach to all their reading. Even good readers need to be exposed to this plan. When she was in seventh grade, Allyson's reading ability was tested and found to be in the post–high school range. Obviously she was a very good reader. Yet after applying SQ3R to her lessons, Allyson commented, "Now this really makes sense. I can see it helping me in science, but I'm using it in social studies, too. It just all connects."

Got the Picture?

Students need the big picture of what we expect them to do when they read their textbooks. By understanding what reading is as it relates to each particular subject, by

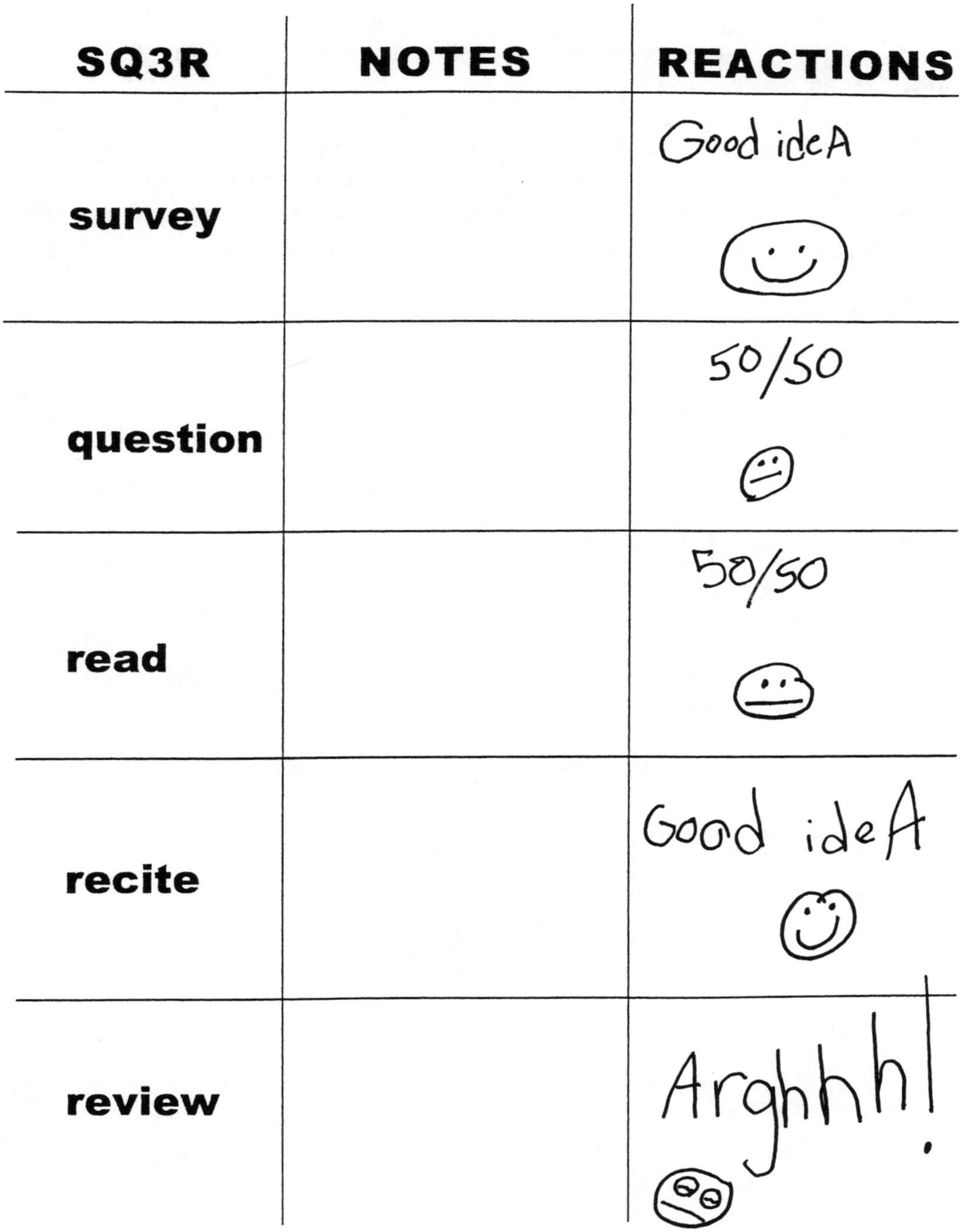

SQ3R	NOTES	REACTIONS
survey		Good ideA ☺
question		50/50 😐
read		50/50 😐
recite		Good ideA ☺
review		Arghhh! 😖

Figure 4–4. *Nick's reactions to SQ3R*

understanding how the texts of that subject are organized, and by developing a plan for the overall approach to studying those texts, all students will be equipped to play on an even field as learners of content.

The big picture is important to establish and reinforce all year long. We believe in sharing accountability across all grades and subjects. We are committed to engaging students, cross-curricularly, in the *processes* of reading; *modeling* the behavior we want to engender; and helping them become *strategic* learners not just for today but for a lifetime. There is, however, the matter of getting through each day's lesson.

CHAPTER 5

MAKING READING HAPPEN: BEFORE

Over the decades we've been exposed to a host of frameworks for creating daily lessons in which students are expected to make meaning from our texts, lectures, and videos. The directed reading activity (Betts 1946), the instructional framework (Herber 1970, Vacca and Vacca 1996), the directed reading-thinking activity (Stauffer 1975), lesson design (Hunter 1984), and many others have been suggested by one well-versed expert after another as ways of presenting material to students in a manner that ensures that all learn. Our favorite is one that, in its simplicity, just makes so much sense—BDA.

BDA in a Nutshell

BDA—Before, During, and After—reminds us that in order for complete transactions with texts to take place, we need to involve students actively *before, during,* and *after* they read, listen, or view. Lytle and Botel (1988, 35) offer the following overview of appropriate activities for each of these phases.

Before Reading

- Linking students' experiences to the text.
- Accessing relevant prior knowledge.
- Acquainting students with the scope and organization of the text before reading it.

During Reading

- Helping students read constructively.
- Helping students use a range of transactions appropriate to the task.
- Capturing initial personal response to the text.

After Reading

- Developing and deepening initial responses to the text.
- Consolidating facts and ideas.
- Connecting with other texts.
- Extending responses.

Typical lessons in our early years of teaching were only *after*. If we had a *before* stage, it was simply to give the assignment, announce the lecture topic, or tell the student seated closest to the light switch to turn off the lights for the video! We hurried students into the *during* stage, imploring them to read the text, listen to the lecture, or view the film. There was always so much to cover! *After* was where we placed our focus. We orchestrated question-and-answer sessions, prepared worksheets, and designed follow-up activities, hoping that our students had read/listened/viewed carefully and skillfully enough to be able to do them. More often than not, only a few responded while the rest seemed disinterested, off base, or terribly confused. We then had to go back, reread it to them, reexplain, retell—in other words, attempt to "repour" our knowledge into their empty heads.

We missed key points of what we now know as BDA lesson design. First, we did not acknowledge the critical importance of what happens *before* the reading/listening/viewing takes place. We did not help students enter the text. We didn't help them make connections between what they already knew and the new information, understand how the text was organized, anticipate what strategies would be needed, and realize the purpose of the transactions we wanted them to make.

Second, we assumed that we had no job to do *during* the time they were expected to absorb our books, lectures, or films. That was *their* job. We failed to guide them in how to do this most effectively given the task at hand. We asked them to dive head first into material without swimming lessons or lifelines. We then spent enormous amounts of time *after* the reading/listening/viewing trying to resuscitate the lesson with rereading, reteaching, and "repouring."

Overall, we missed the most important point, that our job was to create conditions and structures for reading/listening/viewing that would engage all students *actively* in making meaning from our lessons. When we reconceptualized lesson design according to BDA, we found that the *after* stage goes much more quickly, not to mention more successfully, when we spend time facilitating the processes of learning *before* and *during*.

Real teachers are probably wondering where they will find the extra time to spend on *before* and *during*. There is no doubt that time is our archenemy. However, how we spend the time we have is up to us. A BDA focus merely shifts the time used *after* to *before* and *during*. The large amount of time formerly spent spoon-feeding afterward is no longer necessary because the *before* and *during* activities equip students for under-standing.

This chapter and the next two present specific strategies for the *before, during*, and *after* stages of reading. There are naturally many science examples, since that's what Roberta teaches. But don't worry. Teachers in content areas from A to Z—accounting to zoology, and everything in between—have adapted these techniques and found that they work. Over the past twenty-three years, teachers have used them in both hetero-geneous and homogeneous classrooms: in grades K–12; with students labeled academi-cally talented, learning disabled, educable mentally retarded, Chapter I readers, and at-risk; and even with students with no labels at all. No matter where you teach, no matter the type and number of your students, teaching the process, modeling how to do it, and varying strategies will help you meet the real needs of your students.

Tapping into What They Already Know

The impact of spending time on *before* activities was driven home to Roberta by one seventh-grade class and a student teacher, Scott. As they outlined their plans for the day, Roberta cautioned Scott about one aspect of the lesson:

> Watch when I give the homework assignment on classification. All the students have to do is examine the four characteristics listed, exclude the one that doesn't match the others, and then analyze the remaining clues to give the proper phylum or class of the animal described. Sounds simple to me, but they just don't understand what to do. I must not explain it well, either, because I'll go over the first problem with them but will also have to do several more before they know how to proceed.

After teaching her lesson, Roberta settled in to observe Scott teach the next class, fully expecting the same problem with the homework assignment. To her amazement, they breezed through it easily. How did Scott make the homework crystal clear with-out having to repeat himself or go through more than one example? He sang the *Sesame Street* song, "Three of these things belong together, one of these things just doesn't be-long." All students nodded in recognition, knew what to do, and found the assignment easy because Scott remembered to link the new to the known *before* he gave the assignment. (Needless to say, Roberta now always sings when she introduces that assignment!)

Here's another example. Teaching the unseeable is not easy. Atoms and radio waves are harder to understand than bones and seeds that can be seen and touched. Roberta found that the reflection of light rays was difficult for many eighth graders to imagine—until she applied some *before* strategies. Now, each February, Roberta enters class bounc-ing a basketball and asks for a volunteer to join her. As they bounce the ball back and forth, Roberta talks with the class:

ROBERTA: If I bounce this ball to my partner at a high angle, how will it bounce up?

A STUDENT: At a high angle. [They bounce the ball in this manner.]

ROBERTA: What if I bounce it in at a low angle?

A STUDENT: It will go up at a low angle. [The ball is bounced several times to prove this; students predict the correct angle every time.]

ROBERTA: So, you're telling me that we can always predict at what angle this ball will bounce up?

A STUDENT: Yes, the angles in and out are the same.

ROBERTA: The angle going in equals the angle going out?

A STUDENT: Yes.

ROBERTA: Scientists use this same idea when they talk about light rays. Instead of saying that the angle going in equals the angle going out, they try to make it sound more scientific. The angle going in is called the angle of incidence and the angle going out is the angle of reflection. Therefore, the angle of incidence is equal to the angle of reflection. How many of you like to play basketball? [Usually two thirds of the students raise their hands.] Don't you usually use the backboard when you shoot a layup?

A STUDENT: [Nods.]

ROBERTA: The same rule applies. The angle going into the backboard equals the angle going out. You'd better make sure that your angle out (your reflection angle) goes through the hoop or you'll never score. [Eyes widen as the new connection is made.] Thinking of science can make you a better basketball player, and I want you all to remember this—the angle going in equals the angle going out, the angle of incidence is equal to the angle of reflection. Be sure that when you shoot the ball, you have laid it in at the angle you need for it to bounce back through the hoop. Also, be sure to tell your coach that science class has improved your game! [Groans and moans from the kids.] Anyone here like to shoot pool? [About one quarter of the hands go up.] What does this talk of angles and basketball have to do with a pool game?

A STUDENT: Is it with shooting the ball off the side?

ROBERTA: Yes! Don't you predict where the ball should go before you shoot it off of the side? Without knowing the correct language, didn't you already know that the angle of incidence equals the angle of reflection every time you make a bank shot? [Nods.] In what other game can this knowledge be useful?

A STUDENT: Air hockey uses this idea for bank shots! Ping pong and tennis angles can be predicted!

Using five games her students know, Roberta taps into their prior knowledge to help them understand invisible light rays *before* they use their textbooks and labs. With the stage set, a once difficult lesson becomes quite easy.

Accessing prior knowledge has been likened to *building bridges from the known to the new* and *accessing the file folders of the mind* (Anderson and Pearson 1978, 1984, Dole et al. 1991, Tompkins 2001). As real—and sometimes messy—teachers, we can relate to the file folders metaphor. If you came to us and said, *Hey, Donna and Roberta, I read your book and was inspired to create this great activity for my students. I wrote it up and want to give you a copy*, we would of course thank you profusely. But what happened next would be significant. If we took your activity and tossed it in the general direction of our filing cabinet, it would fall to the floor, be swept out with the trash, and we'd never see it again. However, if we went to the filing cabinet, pulled out the appropriate folder, and put your activity into it, we would have your work forever.

All the experiences of one's life are stored in the mind in the equivalent of mental file folders. In order to "insert" new information, we must help our students open their minds, pull out the appropriate "folders," and make connections with things they already know. We so often forget to do this, or we make such connections *after* the reading is done under the guise of "extension," "application," or "enrichment." Perhaps we use our testing posture more often than our teaching posture. A teaching posture requires that we move the personal connections forward *before* the reading takes place so that students can make meaning right from the start. After determining what is central for students to understand from any of our texts—printed, spoken, or pictorial—our next question should be, *What do they already know that I could use as a hook to engage them actively in this text?* That's clearly teaching-posture-type thinking. But that's our job, isn't it?

Getting students to access prior knowledge can be as easy as writing down a few words or sentences based on the lesson of the day. For example, one worksheet that Roberta uses at the start of the school year begins: "You probably heard about cells in science class last year. *Before* you start to read, write three complete sentences about cells." This introductory task gets the mind working, helps define the topic, and taps prior knowledge; the student finds it easier to proceed.

Risk Taking Up Front

Several years ago, Donna attended a workshop dealing with strategies for comprehending across the curriculum. It was conducted by Dorsey Hammond (Hammond 1985). The workshop was wonderful—a whole day of stimulating ideas for teaching. However, by three o'clock in the afternoon, here is what was going through Donna's mind: *I'm tired— on overload with great ideas—I have a grad school final exam on school law tonight at 6:00— what is tort liability, anyway?—what is the quickest route between this workshop and my grad class two hours away?* Don't misunderstand. Dorsey Hammond is an enthusiastic work-shop leader and it was a very worthwhile day, but by three o'clock, Donna was tired of sitting, mentally drained, and preoccupied by other significant events in her life. (In other words she was feeling a lot like many students who sit in our classes!)

At three o'clock, Dorsey said, "Next, we're going to read an informational article about crocodiles!" and Donna thought, *Oh, no, I should have left at the break.* Dorsey continued, "Get a partner and make a list of everything you know about crocodiles!" Donna turned to her partner and said, "I don't know anything about crocodiles and am not sure I want to." Her partner turned out to be a surprising storehouse of informa-tion about these beasts. Donna's interest was piqued by the things she heard. (Amazing what students can learn from one another if we allow them to collaborate.) As the room full of partners compiled their lists, Dorsey visited each pair briefly. To Donna he said, "Tell me something else you think you know about crocodiles." Donna replied, "Oh, I don't know anything else." He persisted. "I know you think you don't, but take a guess." Donna, not knowing any "correct" facts, wouldn't answer. Dorsey prompted, "Well, how about their size?" Donna wouldn't even guess. "Well, are they bigger than three feet?" And Donna said, "Oh. I think so." "Great!" said Dorsey, "Write that guess down on your list!" and off he went. He continued from pair to pair, prompting and probing, getting each pair to risk a guess about what was going to be in the article. When he was fin-ished he said, "Go down your list, put a check beside anything you're sure of, a ques-tion mark beside anything you're not sure of, and go ahead and read!"

When Donna got to the paragraph about the size of crocodiles, the information leaped off the page. She didn't care to know it then, does not really want to know it now, but is certain that only death will take from her the knowledge that crocodiles grow to between nine and twelve feet long if left unhunted in their habitats. What made this knowledge stick even though Donna, like some of our students, wasn't at all interested in the subject or at her peak of concentration? She was forced to become actively in-volved with reading *before* it began. She was forced to take a risk, to guess, to experi-ence disequilibrium with information of which she was not certain. She had made a commitment about the size of crocodiles and her mind wanted to know if it was right.

How often do we allow this disequilibrium, this guessing and risk taking, to occur in school? Don't we typically convince students *not* to take risks? that correct answers are required all of the time? not to guess? Certainly, we do strive for correct answers. The question is *when?* *After* reading, listening, viewing, and their related discussions, we want our students to know the content of our lessons. However, if we take time to set up an environment that encourages risk taking—best-guessing based on what they already know—*before* reading/listening/viewing, we may just find that the important information we have to teach will "stick."

Things We Know, Things We Think We Know But Are Not Sure, Things We Don't Know

Roberta likes to apply this technique to her introduction of a unit on annelids (segmented worms, specifically earthworms). Using another variation suggested by Dorsey Hammond, she asks students to fold a piece of paper into three vertical columns with the following headings: Things We Know; Things We Think We Know But Are Not Sure; Things We Don't Know. Students think about earthworms and, individually, fill in the three columns. As Roberta circulates, she offers encouragement to those afraid to put down answers that aren't "correct." (Many students need to be assured that taking risks like this is acceptable.) This could easily be done as a whole-class discussion, but Roberta wants everyone to write—that way, *everyone* is actively involved, not just the four or five who like to participate in and dominate discussions. She also finds that writing the answers first removes much of the fear of voicing them; therefore, when the discussion does begin more people participate.

Once everyone has finished, students share ideas and collate their work on the board. The give-and-take as students debate the proper placement of information is interesting. Students teach one another (and Roberta) new ideas as they work it through. When they have finished, a volunteer scribe copies the information and gives it to Roberta. Reading over the columns, she points out that it's a waste of precious time to deal with information in the first column; the class already has agreed that they know and understand it. The items in the second and third columns, however, identifying things students don't know and think they need to know, will dictate Roberta's job over the next three weeks. Student empowerment! Because they have contributed to the course of action, they are much more willing to delve into the subject. Periodically, Roberta publicly refers back to this page so students can sees she is following their mandate. As an added benefit, everyone has a review outline in hand at the end of the unit.

This three-column technique is similar to Ogle's K-W-L (1986), which asks students to think about what they *know* in the first column, what they *want to learn* in the second, and what they *learned* in the third. Both approaches are useful to help students identify their collective knowledge or lack thereof. A unit on a topic about which students have little background requires a slightly different approach. When students find that they *know* very little before reading, Roberta reassures them that it's okay not to know *yet* and talks with them about how to tackle information that is so new. The end result? Students are much more willing to slow down their reading rate and learn new strategies for reading difficult text. (We discuss this more fully in Chapter 6.)

Comparing Prior Knowledge Before the Equipment Gets Broken

Getting middle school students to take risks is not easy. Many pupils refuse to write down an answer unless they know it to be true. Is this a conditioned reflex from our profession's emphasis on *after* activities where answers are graded? Probably. By conducting *before* activities where incorrect answers are acceptable as "best guesses so far," students become more willing to take risks and try to forge connections on their own. Roberta handles these activities in her class through small-group discussion followed by whole-class discussion.

For example, students come to her class with varying degrees of prior knowledge about microscopes but with a great deal of interest in using them. Some of them are familiar with expensive microscopes, some have seen only the toy variety or none at all. Before she introduces the parts and proper use of the microscopes, Roberta has her students work in groups of four to compare their "best guesses" to six discussion questions about proper handling of microscopes:

1. Where do you put your specimen on a microscope? Why?
2. How many eyes should you keep open when using a 'scope? Why?
3. Describe how to carry a microscope safely.
4. What does coarse mean when spelled C-O-A-R-S-E?
5. How do you focus a microscope?
6. What is lens paper used for?

Roberta gives the groups six minutes to discuss how they *think* the microscope should be used. She invites "experts" in the class to share their knowledge with novice users. During group discussions, she does not declare novices' incorrect answers as "wrong," but works with them to build common knowledge. Working as cooperative communicators, they reach consensus about the best way to handle these expensive pieces of equipment. In addition to preparing them for subsequent reading, discussing, viewing, and doing, these discussions give Roberta a window into her students' background knowledge—as fine or as poor as that may be. Each time, she becomes better able to plan and pace her future lessons. And—not as much equipment gets broken in the process!

Word Webs

Having trouble getting your students to tap into what they already know? Do they think that because it's new subject matter, they don't have any prior knowledge? Are they intimidated by the subject or afraid to take risks? *Word webbing* is one possible solution.

Michael

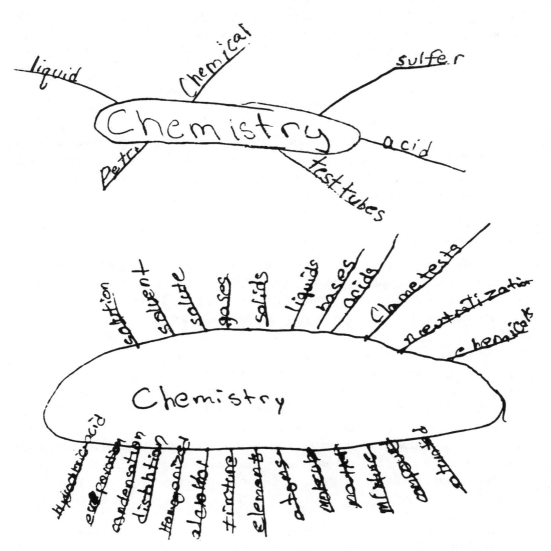

Figure 5–1. *Before and after chemistry word webs*

In word webbing, the topic under study is placed in the center of the web. Students brainstorm their associations with the topic on web strands surrounding it.

Roberta uses a word web as an icebreaker on the first day of school by asking her students to brainstorm their present and past associations with chemistry, the first topic of the year. Typical initial associations are "test tubes," "chemicals," and "experiments." After six weeks of reading, writing, and experimenting, she asks them to repeat the web. Mike's examples (Figure 5–1) are typical. Before the unit, he was building on a layman's knowledge. However, that's what he knew—and that was fine with Roberta. He was able to complete the second web within minutes, demonstrating greater and more sophisticated knowledge by using such words as "tincture," "homogenized," "saturated," and "solvent." When students view their before and after understanding side-by-side and see the progress they have made, their confidence and self-esteem increase.

The same technique can be used in the course of a single lesson, as Roberta has done with a video on the disease hepatitis (see Figure 5–2). By giving students the same web to complete before and after viewing, students receive immediate feedback on what they have learned. When used as a whole-class activity, with the teacher or a student transcribing the information generated by the class, webs can spark discussion and debate at all points in a lesson or unit.

The Power of Prediction

One of Roberta's favorite ways to draw students into a lesson is to have them predict word meanings before they encounter them in their texts. She lifts the words and a bit of the context in which they appear and has students predict their meaning based on a combination of their prior knowledge and the clues they get from the context (see Figure 5–3).

Before reading four pages about algae in their text, students are asked to think about what they will read by filling in the Meaning Before Reading column. This is risky for many students, who balk at writing answers of which they aren't sure. However, it is important to concentrate on the skill of discovering word meanings through content-area context, not just as a separate lesson in English class. (Roberta is sharing account-ability with other teachers here.) She circulates to encourage students to hypothesize when they draw a blank with a word. Finally, she models the reasoning that can be used to guess—to take a risk, to set up disequilibrium so that learning can take place—even when it's a bad guess:

ROBERTA: Pyrenoid is a new word to most of us, isn't it? [Nods.] What do you do when you come across a new word?

A STUDENT: You can break it apart.

ROBERTA: That's what I do with this word. *Pyre* makes me think of pyromaniac,

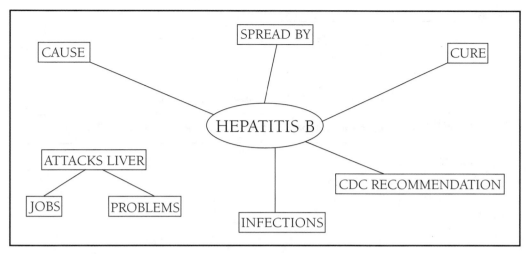

Figure 5–2. *Variation of word webs*

someone who likes to start fires, and *noid* reminds me of that character on the pizza commercials. So, *pyrenoid* makes me think of torching that noid!

A STUDENT: But that can't be the right answer!

ROBERTA: I know, but does anyone have a better idea? [Heads shake.] Then, that's our best guess so far, isn't it?

[Pyrenoids, by the way, are starch-containing bodies in the cells of algae.]

After completing the first column, students begin to read, already alerted to key topics. Next, they complete the Meaning After Reading column and discuss their work. Most students are able to recognize that *holdfast* means to stick (like strong glue) and thus are able to infer in the reading that holdfasts in algae act similarly to roots. All of Roberta's most recent 225 seventh graders predicted that *cast* meant the hard object used by doctors on broken bones and were surprised to find it meant coloring. All but one of these 225 were able to break apart *unicellular* into *one cell*. (Marti had *fat* on her mind and thought of *cellulite*!) Reading *alga*, most students think they are catching a spelling mistake in the text. This, once again, leads Roberta into sharing accountability for teaching as she talks about scientific terminology—use of Latin singular (*alga*) and plural (*algae*) nouns. Most recognize *filament* as the root in *filamentous*. *Blades* connotes the cutting edge to students but actually is the flat edge. For those who have music class before science, *conducting tissue* is very perplexing. They can't seem to mix the images of orchestra conductor and toilet paper! Roberta finds that by using this worksheet in one forty-three-minute class period, students both understand and remember the content.

Scientist _____

Reference: *Foundations*, pp. 150-153

MEANING BEFORE/ MEANING AFTER

Word	Meaning Before Reading	Meaning After Reading
called <u>holdfasts</u>		
a green <u>cast</u>		
<u>unicellular</u>		
very tiny <u>alga</u>		
<u>filamentous alga</u>		
called <u>pyrenoids</u>		
leaflike <u>blades</u>		
<u>conducting</u> tissue		
<u>complex</u> process		

Figure 5–3. *Predicting word meaning*

Dianne, our art teacher colleague, takes this activity one step further when she adds a third column asking them to illustrate the underlined word. Can't you see this being adapted to teaching social studies (words like *monopoly, tariff, blitzkrieg*), Shakespeare (*ducdame, exeunt, intendment*), or geometry (*theorem, congruent, geodesic*)? By setting the stage for the reading—getting students to think, take risks, and make predictions—new words and concepts are assimilated more easily into a meaningful context. Lessons do not need to be repeated because students are actively engaged with their text before they read it.

You may wish to alert students to new ideas with a very simple, one-minute prediction activity that "sets the mood" for the reading assignment. Roberta uses the exercise in Figure 5–4 to introduce a chapter assignment on heat and temperature. She asks students to think about words they will encounter in their reading and make some preliminary distinctions among them. She also spells out the purpose for the reading.

Another way to help students become strategic readers is to ask them to make predictions, read, and then try to verify their hypotheses. Social studies teacher Brendan uses a predict-read-prove format (Figure 5–5) with his seventh-grade classes. Again, *before* the reading begins, students sift through their prior knowledge while they evaluate the new vocabulary. Hoping to be proven correct, they slow down their reading as they search for these words and their meanings.

Roberta uses this technique to deal with more than just new vocabulary. Using the time-honored true/false mode, she engages students in predictions about key concepts before they read them in their books. And why limit this activity just to reading?

HEAT AND TEMPERATURE

Underline the words that you think can go with the word *temperature*.

heat	boiling	energy	matter

speed   freezing

Now circle those words that you think can go with the word *heat*. Have you circled and underlined the same words?

In this chapter, you will learn that heat and temperature ARE NOT the same. When you are finished with the reading guide, come back to this section and review your choices. Have you changed your mind about some of the words? Be prepared to give your reasons.

Figure 5–4. *Setting the mood for reading*

PREDICT

   This section contains many terms that are important to understanding the meaning of the chapter. Below is a list of these terms. *Before reading the selection* (pages 131–135), see if you can *predict* the meanings from the list and place them in the blanks that you think fit the definitions below the word list.

WORD LIST

a. middle ages

b. medieval period

c. dark ages

d. manors

e. feudalism

f. lords

g. vassal

h. fief

i. nobility

DEFINITIONS

1. A system of government and land holding in which one powerful man owned large estates, had his own army, and administered the laws for the people on his estates.

   _____

2. The term for the all-powerful man who owned the large estates.

   _____

3. A period of violence, confusion, and disorder.

   _____

4. Large estates.

   _____

5. The two terms that apply to western Europe at the passing of the Roman Empire when a new civilization was taking shape.

   _____ and _____

6. Members of the upper class.

   _____

7. A man who was given some land with the promise of protection in return for certain duties.

   _____

Figure 5–5. *Predict, read, prove*

Listening and viewing present students with "texts" with which to interact to establish meaning. The sheet in Figure 5–6 focuses students' attention on a video rather than allowing them to sit back passively and daydream. In addition, this can become a quick tool for evaluating students' grasp of new information as they predict-view-prove.

Placing time and emphasis on prediction is important not only for transactions with texts but also for hands-on work. Learning in labs, shops, home-economics rooms, and technology and computer centers becomes more meaningful when we engage students in *before* activities. As Roberta's students learn to use metric lab equipment, she routinely asks them to estimate measurements before using the equipment. In this way, they are encouraged to think "metric" rather than use English-to-metric conversions. Next, students measure and evaluate their predictions.

It is standard for science experiments to ask for hypotheses before experimentation begins. By nature, an experiment is an exercise in *predict-do-prove*. The same is true for English teachers who ask students to predict the endings of chapters and stories. We need to recognize the power that prediction holds for other than its traditional uses and make it part of our standard lesson design.

Visualizing Directions Before the Fingers Get Burnt

Real teachers know all too well the frustration when students don't follow directions. (Some students even admit that they skip directions!) Frustration escalates to potential danger in a science lab. Teachers of technology, consumer sciences, and vocational courses also know that the ability to follow directions is vitally important when dealing with expensive and/or dangerous equipment.

Caution is always the watchword when Roberta's experiments deal with middle school students and fire. One year she and reading specialist Lucy cotaught a class of students who were labeled "slow readers" and "learning disabled." They had tried many approaches to get these students to follow directions in lab. Nothing had worked well, and the experiment with fire was next. Then Roberta remembered that poor readers often do not visualize when they are reading. So she had her students read the directions and draw them on their lab page *before* they could begin the experiment. Figure 5–7 shows the set of directions and the students' renderings of them.

Take a good look at their work. Only two students were able to render the directions correctly. Can you figure out which two? Students 2 and 5 depict a cup and a beaker rather than a test tube. Students 4, 6, and 7 show the use of alcohol burners rather than candles. Ouch! We can only guess that students 7, 8, and 11 knew magic, as their test tubes seem to be levitating in thin air! Sadly, students 3, 4, and 6 will need to visit the nurse for their burns. Only students 9 and 12 drew the correct, moreover *safe,* positions.

Science 7: Animals   Zoologist _____

invertebrates

Directions: BEFORE viewing the video, read over these
statements and check those that you think are true. AFTER
viewing, check those that you know are true.

BEFORE   AFTER

_____   _____   1. Ninety percent of all animals on this
                           earth are invertebrates.
_____   _____   2. Invertebrates have a nerve cord
                           surrounded by a backbone.
_____   _____   3. Most invertebrates are small.
_____   _____   4. The largest invertebrates live in the
                           sea because the water helps support
                           their size.
_____   _____   5. Daphnia are microscopic water fleas.
_____   _____   6. Jellyfish are carnivores (meat eaters).
_____   _____   7. Many invertebrates produce great
                           numbers of eggs to ensure that some
                           offspring will survive.
_____   _____   8. Ascaris worms are saprophytes living
                           in humans.
_____   _____   9. Giant sting rays are the largest
                           invertebrates living in the oceans.
_____   _____   10. Starfish are now called sea stars.

_____   _____   11. The chemical calcium carbonate is
                            found in sand at beaches and forms
                            the rock called sandstone.
_____   _____   12. All of the invertebrates found at the
                            bottom of the ocean weigh less than
                            all of the fish in the ocean.

13. Should we try the earthworm experiment shown in the
    video?

14. Try to identify the invertebrates pictured on this page.

Figure 5–6.   *Predict, view, prove*

VISUALIZING DIRECTIONS

Fill a test tube about 2/3 full of water. Hold the test tube with your fingers at the
BOTTOM and slant the test tube with the surface of water over a CANDLE flame for
about a minute.

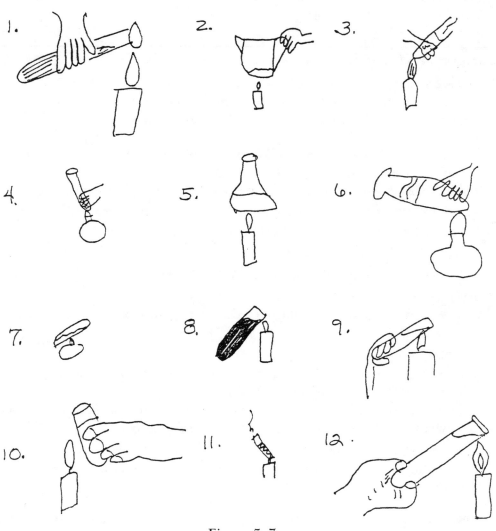

Figure 5–7.

This activity was a real eye-opener for Roberta and Lucy. It also was the moment when things began to change for the better in that class. They began to include more activities that made students picture the words they were reading. They changed labs in order to have the space and time necessary to illustrate directions before starting the activities. Labs did not start until the visualization was on target. The dynamics and safety in that class improved dramatically.

Cartoons and Comics

Cartoons and comics can provide an easy (and friendly) introduction to a lesson. To introduce a unit on fungi, Roberta projects a cartoon on the screen showing a woman in a laundry room and engages her students in a discussion like this:

ROBERTA: Who can tell us what is happening in this cartoon?

A STUDENT: She's getting clothes out of the dryer.

ROBERTA: How do you know it's the dryer? That information isn't given.

A STUDENT: Because it opens in the front, not on the top. Most dryers open in the front.

ROBERTA: Okay, I'll accept that. What else can you tell me?

A STUDENT: The clothes are still wet.

ROBERTA: How many of you agree? How do you know?

A STUDENT: Because mildew doesn't form on dry clothes.

ROBERTA: Is it fair to say that mildew needs warmth and moisture as conditions for growth?

A STUDENT: Yes.

ROBERTA: What is another requirement for the growth of mildew? [It takes some thinking and conversing before someone finally says *darkness*.] There is one other condition that is necessary. [When no one can provide the correct answer, Roberta provides a clue.] Remember, fungi are *not* classified as plants.

A STUDENT: They need food!

ROBERTA: Right. Now, who can list the four conditions needed for the growth of mildew?

Roberta and the students next talk about how *all* fungi need these conditions. By this point, students are prepared to integrate new information into an existing framework of fungi knowledge. The information is more meaningful and more easily remembered when time is spent accessing preexistent knowledge.

Gary Larson's *The Far Side* makes it easy for biology teachers to find pertinent cartoons. However, when you begin looking, you can find comics on almost any subject. (We regularly clip and save comics on math, writing, research papers, etc., finding

Charles Schulz's *Peanuts*, Bil Keane's *The Family Circus*, Batiuk's *Funky Winkerbean*, and Bill Watterson's *Calvin and Hobbes* especially useful.) Libraries contain such treasures as *A Cartoon History of United States Foreign Policy 1776–1976* (Foreign Policy Associates 1976) that display the work of satirists, cartoonists, political commentators, and more throughout American history. (Helpful hint: the editorial page of the daily newspaper treats current events that are relevant in many content areas.) Once you spread the word, students will start bringing in their favorites. Comics grab their attention and interest while stimulating thought and discussion *before* the reading begins.

A Change of Posture: *Teacher* not *Tester*

These *before* activities represent a change in the way we think of our jobs. They remind us that our job is to *teach*. So you're saying, *Well, no kidding*. Bear with us. When we ignored the *before* stage of reading, rushed students through the *during* stage, and focused all our attention on the *after* stage, we were working from the posture of tester, not teacher. Our stance was something like this: *Here's the assignment. Go read it, then we'll ask you questions to see if you got it. If you didn't, there must be something wrong with you. Maybe you weren't paying attention. Maybe you didn't concentrate hard enough. Maybe you should be tested—labeled—sent to a special class—*. This testing posture was not a conscious stance, but one that reflected our own experiences in recitation-oriented classes. We tended to teach the way we were taught, a way that had worked for us.

A teaching posture, on the other hand, takes the time to equip students with the strategies needed to read, listen, or view successfully *before* the assignment, so that the reading, listening, or viewing are more successful for *all* students, not just those who are able—like we were—to be successful on their own. *Before* activities level the playing field, welcoming everyone into the conversations and learning in our classrooms. That way the *after* stage moves much more quickly and is filled with more lively and inclusive discussions.

CHAPTER 6

MAKING READING HAPPEN: DURING

One day Donna asked Roberta's seventh-grade science students what it was like to read in science. To her surprise, they said it was easy. Since she has horrible memories of reading science materials, she asked why they found it so easy. One young lady—not one with a history of success in reading in other classes—said, "Well, Mrs. McManus shows us what the important stuff is. After all, we're not scientists or anything."

Donna had to laugh, remembering the first time Roberta asked her building reading specialist (another Donna) and her to help create a reading guide for a chapter in her seventh-grade science text. Both Donnas took the book home and read the chapter. Then they read it again—and again. The next day each of them said to Roberta, "I don't get it." Roberta said, "Don't get *what*?" The Donnas replied, "*Any* of it." Everyone was surprised. After all, both Donnas had master's degrees *in reading* at the time. How could they have difficulty with a seventh-grade science text? Roberta had skimmed the chapter and found it extremely easy. What was going on here? The notions of schema and readability hit home.

Familiarity and Friendliness

Roberta brought her schema, her prior knowledge of science from years of study, to her reading of this text. The subject was familiar; as a matter of fact, she knew a great deal more than the text actually told. The Donnas, on the other hand, had not studied science since the sophomore year of college. They could pronounce the words with no difficulty, but the gaps in their knowledge interfered with their reading. Their lack of familiarity was compounded by the unfriendly structure of the textbook.

Lytle and Botel (1988) have this to say about textbooks:

Most of the texts either grossly oversimplify concepts and relationships so that readers are forced to make giant leaps and assumptions, or they overwhelm the reader with facts, and teachers struggle to "cover" material that comes with detailed, factual end-of-the-chapter tests and checkouts. (44)

We realize that we are "preaching to the choir" here. Real teachers, we know that you, too, face the textbook conundrum every day. In some ways, we love our texts. After all, who would want to be a first-year teacher again, walk into her classroom, and be told, *Sorry, there are no textbooks for your courses. So just find some material to use, okay?* If there weren't things like textbooks, we'd probably invent them. But we also hate them. Somehow they never completely suit. They're too hard, too easy, too superfluous on some concepts, too in depth on others. They cover only half of what we want to teach, or they cover things we either don't have time or don't want to teach. If we have a locally developed curriculum, published textbooks never seem to match it. If we buy a book and let it become the curriculum, we feel compromised. And whatever we do, we're faced with a very expensive investment for which to stand accountable.

The American Association for the Advancement of Science (AAAS) studied science textbooks and described them as having "no more material about a concept than you would find in a dictionary, and often it's not even that good" (Jehlen 2000, 29). In defense of textbook companies, however, AAAS went on to note that "they're trying to sell to every school district in the United States, and each state has its own standards. As long as the states say they must have all the concepts, we're pushing for a dictionary approach" (29).

Certainly, many factors come into play in the creation of textbooks. Early on in our work together, we read an article by Connie Muther (1985) in which she summarized these factors in one sentence:

> Adoption states, special interest groups, and readability formulas have all contributed to produce textbooks designed by a committee, written by a committee, and selected by a committee to please all and offend none. (7)

It is not easy to meet the preferences of so many constituencies. However, we find it ironic that readability is named as a culprit. Most of us would agree that something is "readable" if it makes sense—that is, if it is comprehensible. However, grade-level readability of text is determined by readability formulas, most of which measure two things: average length of sentences and relative difficulty of words (Dale and Chall 1948, Spache 1953, Fry 1977). These formulas do not measure comprehensibility directly. Of course, one could infer that a passage with long sentences and hard words would be more difficult to understand than one with short sentences and easy words. However, consider this sentence: *I wanted to go home, but I had to go to the store.* This is readable, meaning-wise, isn't it? You can envision a real teacher at the end of a school day who wants desperately to go home, put her feet up, and relax, but she has no food in her house for dinner and must stand in line at the supermarket before ending her day. Now get ready for a surprise. If you want to lower the readability score of this sentence, as measured by a readability formula, this is what you must do: *I wanted to go home. I had to go to the store.*

If we equate readability with comprehensibility, which of these examples is more readable? You probably chose the first, because it has that very important coordinating conjunction *but* that shows the pivotal relationship between the clauses. In order to score lower on a measure of sentence length, however, *but* must be removed, and the longer sentence made into two shorter ones. Those who have stakes in selecting textbooks for adoption invariably want to know, *What is the readability score?* The answer is not so simple. Ironically, the very words that create comprehensibility sometimes are eliminated in order to achieve a lower readability score.

Let's return to the Donnas' dilemma with the seventh-grade science textbook. Their problems stemmed not from a hidden reading disability but from unfamiliarity with the subject and difficulty with an unfriendly text. Asking the Donnas to read her science texts definitely was an eye-opener for Roberta. She saw how even two educated adults could drown in the multitude of facts and generalities in her texts, unable to sort out the more important from the less important. Their reaction alerted her to places where her students were likely to have trouble as well. It helped her see what was not explained well in the texts and to understand the difficulties her students encountered. After all, if this was a problem for the Donnas, how many seventh and eighth graders experienced it too? If you want a sense of how easy your textbook is to read, ask a colleague whose expertise is in a different subject!

For years, Roberta stuck closely to the district-adopted science textbooks, believing that the readability level of outside primary source material was too high for her middle schoolers. In doing so, she severely limited the reading material available to her twelve-to-fourteen-year-olds. A quote by Lytle and Botel (1988) changed her thinking:

> Clearly we should be concerned primarily about the quality of material we ask students to read and the nature of the activities they engage in with text, and much less concerned with specific levels of text difficulty or readability per se. (28)

This emphasis on quality and active engagement liberated Roberta to incorporate more advanced material into her classes rather than rely only on readability-controlled text materials. She refers to this realization as "Freedom with a capital F" to move on to texts that better fit her science topics, such as newspapers, videotapes, pamphlets, websites and magazine articles.

This has required her to change her teaching strategies in the *during* stage of reading to *guide* students in discerning and assimilating new knowledge from these ancillary texts. Roberta finds that her students not only are capable of reading them, they find them to be welcome primary sources to augment and complement their textbooks. However, *guide* is the operative word in the *during* stage.

Reading Guides: The Teacher at Your Side

Roberta tells her students, "My job is not to trick you; my job is to teach you." Her reading guides help her do just that. As their name suggests, they help her guide students through texts. No tricks, no de facto competition to reward the good readers and embarrass the poor ones, just an even playing field for all students. Imagine a classroom where the teacher has the luxury of sitting beside individuals as they read—pointing out the main ideas, reminding them to observe headings and boldface type, suggesting when to speed up or slow down, guiding them in comparing texts to their own experiences. Such utopias are rare in real schools. However, reading guides can create the next best thing by alerting students to key ideas, appropriate strategies, and real-world connections.

There are infinite ways to design a reading guide based on the characteristics of your students and your texts. Wood, Lapp, and Flood overview a number of teacher-tested templates in their book *Guiding Readers Through Texts* (1992). In a sense, reading guides are new and improved versions of the type of "worksheet" Roberta used to give her students when she was operating out of her testing (not teaching) posture. Unfortunately, such worksheets do nothing to further understanding of the text or get students ready to handle more sophisticated ideas. The student's goal is to finish it as quickly as possible.

Reading guides are "front-loaded teaching" rather than the "back-loaded testing" of the sort that went on with worksheets. Rather than completing a worksheet after reading, students use reading guides as the "teacher at their side" before, during, and after the reading. Roberta introduces them as active learning tools to make sure that everyone in the class establishes a common bank of knowledge on which she can expand throughout the unit. She ties them to her purposes for teaching the unit and reassures students that her intention is to "guide," not to "trick."

The first reading guide of the year in Roberta's seventh grade is on cells and structure (see Appendix B, pages 171–73). Roberta lets students work on it in groups of four, easing the pressure to be "good" at reading a new text in a new class and allowing Roberta a peek into the dynamics of the class early on. Having students work in groups right away begins a dialogue that leads into group work and lab work and establishes a sense of community from the beginning of the year. On a more pragmatic note, Roberta likes to have each group submit only one guide for her review, cutting down on the amount of at-home grading she has to do. However, she offers the option of handing in work individually in case members of a group "agree to disagree." As the year progresses and students become more confident readers, they complete them in groups only when the text is more difficult than usual.

Every aspect of Roberta's reading guides is designed to get students actively involved. From the beginning, students are referred to as *cytologists* in the line where *name* usually appears. Over the course of the year, she refers to them as *scientist, mechanic, physicist, geneticist, electrician, pathologist, engineer, chemist, mycologist, zoologist,* and *microbiologist.* In a unit on worms, she even made up the title *wormologist,* much to the groaning amusement of her classes. Any kind of active scientist will do, but they are never, ever called *name!*

The guide for cells and structure is four pages long and covers only eight pages of the text. This is the "hand-holding" reading guide. Roberta is very specific in providing BDA guidance in the same way she would do if she were guiding a group reading of the text. At the beginning of the guide she asks them to access their prior knowledge (*You have probably heard about cells in science class last year. BEFORE you start to read, write three complete sentences about cells*), to notice the text structure (*The "Cells and Structure" section in your book is divided into three subheadings. Please list them*), and to employ the reading strategy she has taught them with a previous piece of text (*Use the SQ3R study plan as you read these pages. Be especially sure to read the questions BEFORE you read each section*).

The guidance *during* reading often includes page numbers, and even paragraph numbers, where information is found. In a text awash with facts and details, this is not a matter of "dumbing down"; it is a matter of guiding students to important information without trying to "trip them up." Remember: Roberta's job is not to trick them but to teach them. In their early experiences in her class, students see this in a direct way.

Roberta varies the types of questions during reading, taking care not to ask only questions that require one-word answers and not limiting her direction to the written text. She also makes sure to call their attention to charts, graphs, and photos. If you have ever watched students read an assignment, you know that it is quite common to see them skip over these important graphic aids. Their attitude seems to be, *Great! Less to read!* Reading guides can correct this problem by asking students questions that relate to these aids.

One example of this in a seventh-grade life science class involved five diagrams on cell division. The text explained the steps of cell division but did not relate them to the diagrams. On her reading guide, Roberta directed the students this way:

> Complete the following diagrams to show cell mitosis in an animal cell. In the blanks next to each drawing, EXPLAIN what is happening at each stage in mitosis. Use your own words.

This was met by consternation. Ariel said, "This is *hard!*" Roberta's response? "But look how well you've done it! By working together, you were able to give great explanations!" When Roberta hears whining and complaining, she knows that students have not made the proper connections between the text and the diagrams. Reading guides force them to slow down their reading, to note graphics, and to assimilate information. They provide an opportunity to insert charts that help the fledgling scientists take pieces of information found separately and integrate them into a meaningful whole. This is how scientists think, and these charts become useful references for future studying.

True to the BDA design, Roberta doesn't end the reading guide with the *during* stage. She includes a short "after reading" section to help students pull their reading together. She has used true/false questions, opinion essays, vocabulary matching, or something as simple as what you see in the cells and structure guide: *Look back to the sentences you wrote for number 1. Would you find it easy to write three more sentences about cells? Try it!* She finds that the *after* stage is a good place to help students make their studies relevant to their lives. (In her opinion, this is easy to do in science.) For example, during a unit on sound, one reading assignment mentioned that a distance of fifty-five feet is necessary for an echo to occur and described hard surfaces versus soft, porous surfaces as "sound reflectors" versus "sound absorbers". Roberta included the following questions at the end of the reading guide: *Why doesn't Mrs. McManus's voice echo in Room 22? Why do some apartment buildings require renters to put carpet on the floors?* Although neither question was addressed directly in the text, Roberta knew that her classroom and the apartment buildings in which many of her students live were rich applications of the concepts. Two simple questions after reading solidified a hard-and-fast, easy-to-remember lesson.

Roberta personalizes these guides for special-needs students in her classes. Many of these students need information chunked, so she often draws a line across a reading guide to separate sections more apparently than just by headings, or she underlines key words in true/false questions. At the beginning of the year, Roberta never sits down while her students are using reading guides. She is always circulating, providing help and support. As the year goes by, she gradually releases control to the students, peering over their shoulders less often. Instead, students come up to her desk for help, or she makes announcements like *I'll be around in ten minutes to answer your questions.* Students respond well to this acknowledgment of their increased abilities to deal with science text independently. She makes sure that she doesn't have them raise their hands to request help. Instead, she talks to everyone individually as she moves through the room giving feedback, not singling out struggling students or poorer readers.

QAD for Success with Fallible Texts

Need a change of pace? Real teachers know that even the best of techniques can become tired, evoking groans and not-this-again moans. So it is with reading guides. QAD: Questions, Answers, and Details (Weehawken Public Schools 1974) is another way to guide reading and is especially useful when students are being eased into independent note taking or when the textbook is murky on some concepts. The basic QAD consists of three columns: in the question column the teacher provides the questions that are relevant to the reading; students write short answers in the answer column and provide details in the details column. The basic QAD format works well when the text is reader friendly. With a minimum of teacher modeling, students are able to locate the answers and supporting details for each question fairly easily. This format helps Roberta lay the groundwork for future discussions about note taking—how to identify what to write down, that note taking does not require complete sentences, that main ideas and details are different, and so on.

Figure 6–1 shows a QAD to accompany a text that is not so straightforward, whose organization is confusing. The QAD she has devised for fungi starts a frank discussion about texts and tasks for reading them:

ROBERTA: Take a look at today's QAD. Tell me how it's different from others that we've used.

A STUDENT: You filled out everything for question 1.

ROBERTA: That's right. I just wanted a quick reminder about what a QAD is. Is this a paper where you need to use complete sentences?

A STUDENT: No. We can use just one or two words for the answers, and phrases for the details.

ROBERTA: That's right, so let's go back to my first question. How is this QAD different? You've told me one way; keep going.

A STUDENT: In numbers 3 and 4, you've told us the answers. Why?

ROBERTA: Because I'm not satisfied with how our book presents this information. It just doesn't jump out at you.

A STUDENT: Is this a mistake in the book?

ROBERTA: No. I just want to be sure that you understand this information. The paragraphs involved here aren't the best. They just list facts without making much of a point. There are no introductory or concluding sentences, just streams of facts. So I want you to understand that for the details on these two questions, you have to give me information about those ideas. However, on the second page of the QAD, I don't have to give you any extra information; you'll supply all of the answers and corresponding details.

Roberta's honesty about the structure of this text lets students in on a little secret of critical reading: texts aren't perfect, and readers need to read with a discerning eye, asking for help when necessary. The scaffold provided by answers, partial answers, and hints builds confidence in reading. Students know that they have an equal opportunity to succeed because their teacher has carefully analyzed their text and empathized with their reading of it.

Our colleague Debbie saw QAD for the first time when she was looking at her son's homework. He was in Roberta's science class and had brought a QAD home. Debbie, a

Science 7

Q	A	D
1. What is QAD?	Question Answer (short) Detail	QAD is a method to take notes. The notes can be taken from a lecture or from a book. So... turn to page 134.
2. To what kingdom do fungi belong?		
3. What are the characteristics of fungi?	a.. many celled b. different cell walls c. cannot make their own food	a. b. c.
4. How do fungi obtain their food?	a. as parasites b. as saprophytes	a. b.
5. How are fungi divided into groups?		examples of fungi:

Figure 6–1. *Page one of two-page QAD*

third-grade teacher, decided that she could adapt this strategy to use with her students. Instead of calling it QAD, she renamed it QAP—Questions, Answers, Pictures. Together, she and her students determine the answers to the questions, then the students draw pictures to illustrate the point. Tweaking another teacher's idea gave QAD a fresh face and a new use with younger students.

We have both used the strategy, in classes from first grade through college, and find it very versatile for guiding reading of textbooks, primary source materials, videos, newspaper and magazine articles, and pamphlets. Roberta sometimes lectures from a QAD that she has prepared for herself, and then shares those notes as a model for note taking (see the example in Figure 6–2). The QAD also comes in handy the next day for a class review and a "catch-up" for absent students. (We will revisit QAD in Chapter 10 as a scaffold for writing.)

Active Involvement Through Charts

As we discussed in Chapter 4, reading is an active process of constructing meaning. You can't get much more active than asking students to read and fill in organizational charts about their reading. (See the example in Figure 6–3.) The vertical and horizontal co-ordinates automatically set reading tasks causing students to search for and compare and contrast information. Instant purpose!

Roberta is able to adapt the assignment in Figure 6–3 for varying levels of ability. Using their text, students should be able to fill in all but two of the squares. In her higher-performing classes, she does not give this information ahead of time; she lets them discover it on their own. She tells middle-level students that there are two boxes that they will not be able to fill in, through no fault of their own. She tells lower-ability classes which two boxes to put Xs through. This leads to conversations about an important lifetime reading skill: recognizing when you need more information than the current text gives and deciding where you might look to find it. Rather than missing this opportunity to help students distill information because the textbook does not cover all the information, or simply supplying the missing information, Roberta uses it as an opportunity to teach reading.

Because Roberta creates her own charts, she can tailor them to any specifications she chooses, thus enabling her to teach opportunistically about science and literacy. The chart in Figure 6–4 asks students to visualize and draw the effect of different types of mirrors, and think of examples of these mirrors in their lives. Rather than remaining unattached from science, students immerse themselves in familiar applications. Reinforcement of literacy concepts sneaks in when Roberta asks her students for *adjectives* to describe types of reflectors and *nouns* to name examples. Her students always are amused that their science teacher knows such words. After all, she teaches *science*.

QAD – Periodic Table
   Q = question
   A = answer
   D = detail

Q	A	D
1. What are "groups" on the table?	VERTICAL COLUMNS	-NUMBERED 1–18 - HAVE SIMILAR ARRANGEMENTS OF ELECTRONS -HAVE SIMILAR PROPERTIES
2. What are "periods" on the table?	HORIZONTAL ROWS	-SAME NUMBERS OF ELECTRON SHELLS - EACH ELEMENT IS IN A DIFFERENT GROUP AND HAS DIFFERENT PROPERTIES
3. Elements on the left side of the chart are ___.	METALS	- 3 OR FEWER ELECTRONS IN THE OUTER SHELL - GOOD CONDUCTORS - MALLEABLE - DUCTILE - GIVE UP ELECTRONS READILY IN REACTIONS
4. What are Group 1 elements?	ALKALI METALS	-SOFT -LOW MELTING POINT -MOST REACTIVE OF ALL METALS - GOOD CONDUCTORS -NOT FOUND FREE IN NATURE
5. What are Group 2 elements?	ALKALINE EARTH METALS	-VERY REACTIVE -SOME REACT WITH WATER

Figure 6–2. *Roberta's notes for a lecture*

Type of Fungus	What is it?	Where is it found?	How is it beneficial to humans?	How is it harmful to humans?	Examples
Sporangium Fungi					
Club Fungi					
Sac Fungi					
Lichen					

Figure 6–3. *A chart to guide reading*

When a reading guide would be too cumbersome or too time-consuming, a *semantic map* can serve as a teacher- and student-friendly way to help students organize the important points of a reading assignment. Texts often become so cluttered with facts that young readers miss the main ideas, seeing the trees but not the proverbial forest. Roberta places a semantic map (see the example in Figure 6–5) on the overhead projector, and students copy it into their notes. When doing their reading, they use this map to organize the information that supports these main ideas. The map also makes students accountable. Roberta simply circulates through the classroom, clipboard in hand, noting who attempted to complete the map. In less than five minutes, she has graded the effort and is ready to lead a discussion to clarify and extend the information.

An advanced level of thinking is required to organize and chart information while reading. Roberta encourages the more challenged students to ask for help rather than become frustrated. To make sure this happens, she circulates through the room, ready to assist. However, they quickly learn that she will not *give* the answers. This distinction is important. She will direct them to a page, a column, or a paragraph, but the final discovery is theirs. Students are willing to search for answers when they feel that they can be successful. Again, they are reading *to learn*, not to be tripped up by a teacher's worksheet. An added bonus is fewer discipline problems. Because they feel they can be successful, they are more willing to try new things rather than find ways to avoid them.

Science 8: Unit 6   Scientist _____

MIRRORS AND REFLECTION

Read page 441 and fill in the following chart.

Reflectors	Types (adjectives)	Examples (nouns)
Poor		
Good		

Read pages 442 - 443. As you go along, fill in the following chart.

Types of mirrors	Drawing	Effect on size (larger, smaller, same)	Effect on position (right side up, upside down)	Type of image (real, virtual)	Examples
Plane					
Convex					
Concave					

Figure 6–4. *Parts of speech in science*

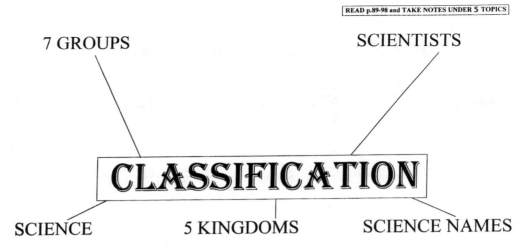

Figure 6–5. *Semantic map to organize information*

No Prior Knowledge? Text Boxes to the Rescue!

By the time Roberta's students arrive in her classes, they have had an initial exposure to most of her curriculum. Her school district spirals science topics in grades K–6 and then invites students to become specialists as they delve deeper into subjects during middle and high school. Real teachers know this is a noble plan, but changing standards, shifts in administration, and curriculum updates create gaps. Sometimes students arrive with *no* prior knowledge to bring to a unit. This happened to Roberta in her unit on genetics and heredity. The information was so foreign to her students she knew her typical reading guides and QADs would not be enough. Reassuring them that their lack of prior knowledge was not their fault, she talked with her classes about how they needed to change their reading approach to this unit. Together they recognized the need to slow down their reading. Roberta remembered some research she and Donna had done with students (Topping and McManus 1993) using a technique they ultimately called text boxes. One thing they found was that the text boxes caused students to slow down their reading, really stopping to monitor their comprehension.

So Roberta created the text boxes shown in Figure 6–6 to help her students meet their goal of reading more slowly. Students agreed to stop at the end of every paragraph and check for comprehension. Like a good coach, Roberta modeled reading the opening paragraphs, thinking aloud some possible notes that she might write, questions and reactions she might jot down in the boxes. Together, the class began the arduous process of reading this difficult text together, using the SQ3R model and making notes at the end of each paragraph.

INHERITANCE BY GENES

PAGE 316

NOTES	REACTIONS
Paragraph 1	
Figure 15–3 and caption	
Paragraph 2	
Figure 15–4 and caption	
Paragraph 3	

Figure 6–6. *Text boxes*

By recording their thoughts, students were making the connections between new and previously known information. By jotting down questions and reactions, they were giving themselves goals to meet as they continued reading. Later, during a class discussion of the material, Roberta wrote students' comments on the overhead. This made sure everyone had the notes they needed to study for quizzes. Afterward, when Roberta asked them to outline the same reading assignment, the students proclaimed it easy. The strategy had worked!

Punctuation Pause

Although most of the reading in Roberta's classroom is done silently, a highly unfamiliar piece (like the one on genetics and heredity) is the perfect opportunity to ask students to read aloud. Reading aloud automatically slows down the reading rate, and giving voice to the print on the page provides another sensory emphasis. (How many times have you stopped and read something aloud because it was complicated and you needed to hear it voiced?)

We're not talking about the round-robin reading of our collective pasts (Optiz and Rasinski 1998)—counting how many people were ahead of you—counting to find the paragraph you would have to read—wishing for a shorter one—practicing that paragraph with a tightening knot in your stomach—finally blurting it out—then sighing with relief or embarrassment when it was over. During the preperformance anxiety and the postperformance letdown of round-robin reading, readers focus little attention on listening and the meaning of the text.

What to do instead? The answer presented itself during a parent-teacher conference, when Roberta was in the parent's chair talking to her son Mark's teacher, Rosemary. After the business of the conference was over, they lapsed into teacher talk. Rosemary described a technique that she was using with her sixth graders that seemed just right. Roberta borrowed it, shared it with Donna, and they gave it a name—*punctuation pause*.

In punctuation pause, students take turns reading, stopping whenever they come to a punctuation mark. Therefore, no one reads more than one sentence, and some read only one word. This delights them! The differences in reading abilities are not so apparent to peers, so anxiety levels plummet. Everyone is dealing with new scientific words, so a blunder is understandable. Let's face it: *phenotype, recessive, Punnett Square*, and *mixed dominance* are not part of most people's daily speaking vocabularies. The novelty of this approach tends to keep students focused. The first year Roberta used this technique, only one out of 128 students lost her place in the text.

Teaching strategies such as text boxes and punctuation pause allows students to encounter difficult material without being intimidated by it. Learning is now within the reach of everyone. Thanks to such techniques, Roberta is able to keep her curriculum updated with formerly too-difficult-for-middle-schoolers primary source material.

Videos, the Internet, newspapers, and magazines regularly update her aging textbooks—a real issue in the rapidly changing field of science.

Virus Partners

One way Roberta adds excitement (yes, excitement) to completing guides is by asking students to work in pairs. Working in pairs often leads to more successful viewing and reading. By nature adolescents are social beings, and as another real teacher, Nancie Atwell, says, "Our teaching can take advantage of this, helping kids find meaningful ways to channel their energies and social needs instead of trying to legislate against them" (1987, 25). Virus Partners (see Figure 6–7) is a way of organizing such pairing.

Roberta, to her students' eye-rolling delight, tells them they will be choosing four partners with whom they will "share viruses" over the next four days. Then students take five minutes to complete the circle and hook it in their notebooks. But Roberta has planned four days in a row of using videos, magazines, and newspaper articles. Each day students enter the classroom and find this message on the board, "Today you are to sit with your A [B, C, or D] partner. If you do not have a partner, stand at the side of the room." It only takes one day for students to adjust. The next day, Roberta typically

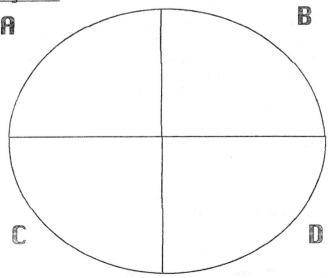

VIRUS PARTNERS!!   You need to get four <u>different</u> people to sign each area of your circle. When someone signs a letter for you, you must sign the SAME letter for them.   Reminder, each person can sign for your circle <u>only once.</u>

Figure 6–7. *Partnering to learn*

walks in to find everyone in their seats. Students announce, "Pam's partner is absent and Tom wasn't here when we picked partners, so we paired them together. Okay?" Planning makes this four-day exercise in viewing, reading, and writing a snap!

The Naked Scientist Mystery

While preparing materials for a unit on density and flotation, Roberta came across the following narration that she thought her students would enjoy.

> Archimedes did much of his work for King Hiero. In one famous story, the king suspected that a goldsmith had not made a new crown of pure gold, but had mixed in some less costly silver. The king asked Archimedes to find out if the goldsmith had cheated. Archimedes found the answer to this problem while taking a bath. His solution rested on *volume* (the amount of space occupied by an object). Archimedes noticed that water spilled out of the bath as he placed his body into it. By measuring the amount of water his body displaced, he could measure its volume. Archimedes was so excited when he found the answer that he ran into the street without dressing, shouting "Eureka!" (I have found it!). Archimedes compared the amount of water displaced by the crown to the amount of water displaced by an equal weight of pure gold. The crown displaced more water, and so it was not pure gold. The goldsmith had cheated (Calinger 1997).

Students read the story and at the end looked, frankly, unimpressed. Their expressions said, *So?* Class after class failed to be interested; even a naked scientist couldn't capture their attention. Roberta was stumped. This slice-of-life story should have been interesting enough to underscore the principles of density and flotation. Why were they not getting it?

The next time, she approached this story as a mystery to be solved—a mystery whose outcome could mean the difference between life and death for the jeweler. Students read one sentence at a time. As the story progressed, Roberta drew pictures of the crown on the board and assigned numerical value to its weight and volume. This time around, students were intrigued. Thanks to the drawings and the measurements, they understood that the jeweler had cheated the king. This led to a discussion of drawing, and how visualizing a situation by sketching can help increase understanding. Roberta was quick to remind them that they would be able to use scratch paper in their upcoming standardized reading tests and that drawing just might be a strategy that would give them the edge.

End-of-the-Year Independence Day

If you remember, Roberta always circles December 13 on her calendar. It is Over-the-Hump Day, the time of the year when she can pick up the pace in her classes (see Chapter 3). If this day deserves a special title, then the day when Roberta introduced her

Science 8: Unit 8   Electrician _____

ELECTRICITY

You will be working at your own speed. Check off each step as you finish.

_____   Do **Experiment #5**. You can find it in your lab kit.

_____   Do **Experiment #6**. It is also found in your lab kits. If you have trouble with the electroscope, let Mrs. McManus know.

_____   **Read** the following questions and then read over pages 11–12 in your book. Answer the questions as you go along.

1. Which atomic particle is exchanged during a chemical reaction?

2. What two metals did Alessandro Volta use in his voltaic cell?

3. What electrolyte did Volta use? (Electrolyte is defined in your vocabulary list.

4. Define electromotive force.

5. Identify the two metals used in a dry cell.

_____   We will do **Experiments #7 & 9** as class activities.

_____   Copy the drawing Figure 19–1 on page 19 into your jottings. **Add arrows** to show the direction and path of the current.

_____   Do **Experiment #8**. It is in a kit on the side counter. You will also need a flask of salt water and a galvanometer. These too are on the side counter.

_____   Do **Experiment #10**. It is set up for you on a front table. Be sure to consult the text to help you with Part IV. Be sure to use complete sentences to write your conclusions.

Figure 6–8.   *Page one of independent work on electricity*

last unit of the eighth-grade curriculum one year surely must be called Independence Day. Roberta had taken her students from total dependence on her in September through a gradual release of that control by teaching them both content and process. She and her students reaped the rewards during the final electricity unit. (We hear you gasp. Electricity?! Independence?! Eighth graders?! End of the year?! Was her liability insurance paid up? Yes to all the above.)

Figure 6–8 is the written guide Roberta gave to her students. Following this self-guided investigation of electricity step by step, they read, interpreted charts, performed labs, analyzed information, and drew conclusions without Roberta's help. They moved around the room, working at their own paces; Roberta served as a consultant.

Ironically, this guide looks very much like the types of worksheets teachers often give *at the beginning of the year*. On close inspection, you can see a lot of assumptive teaching, more of a testing posture than a teaching posture. The difference is this: Roberta had built up to this all year long; she didn't start with it. At this point she found her students needed little intervention from her, which at the end of the year is a good thing. She was freed to do all of those end-of-the-year tasks that real teachers face—inventorying equipment, collecting texts, levying fines, filling out volumes of forms, keeping the lid on the middle school, confiscating water balloons—while meaningful education continued right to the end!

CHAPTER 7

MAKING READING HAPPEN: AFTER

One thing is sure: no teacher likes to find out while grading a quiz or test that her students didn't "get it." You've provided the *before* activities, guided reading well *during*, and now it's time to find out whether they "got it"—before a high-stakes test or quiz comes along. Welcome to some *after* activities that we have found to be quite successful. These activities are engaging and fun, the kinds of things teachers enjoy providing and their students love doing. All too often the "after reading" stage is drudgery—finding out that they haven't read it, didn't understand it, aren't interested, and having to perform academic CPR on lifeless lessons. The key to a fun *after* is having done a good job *before* and *during*.

Pick a Card, Any Card

An easy, simple-to-make game that Roberta's students enjoy is Pick a Card, Any Card. She uses it to review key vocabulary from a passage they have just read. For simplicity's sake, Roberta always limits the cards to eleven so the game can be played in about five minutes. Here's how to set up the cards:

1. On each of ten cards write a vocabulary word that students should have learned from their reading.
2. On the eleventh card, put a star on one side and a definition of any one of the words on the original ten cards on the other side.
3. Now *randomly* write definitions of the other nine vocabulary words on the blank sides of nine of the remaining ten cards. Mix up the definitions so that a definition is not on the same card as the vocabulary word it matches.
4. Confused? Let's recap. You should have nine cards each of which has a vocabulary word on one side and a definition that doesn't match it on the other.

You also should have one card with only a vocabulary word on it. And you should have another card with a definition on one side and a star on the other. (If our math hasn't failed us, that's 9 cards with words and nonmatching definitions + 1 card with a word only + 1 card with a star and a definition = 11 cards altogether.)

You have just survived the nonfun part of this activity: figuring out our directions for a very easy task! Here's how Roberta and her students play. Roberta circulates through the room asking for ten volunteers to "pick a card, any card." She keeps the card with the star and definition herself to start the game. She reads the definition and the student with the matching vocabulary word runs to the front of the room. This student turns his/her card over and reads the definition on the other side. The student with the word that matches that definition runs to the front of the room, turns his/her card over and reads the next definition, and so forth, until all ten words have been matched with their definition.

Each time they play, Roberta uses a stopwatch and notes the time it takes to complete all ten words. She records the times on the board by classes. Students turn this into a friendly competition in two ways. They try to improve their own class's score each time they play, and they try to beat the times of other classes. This is a wonderful activity for middle school students; it tunes into their natural competitiveness at this age, and it allows them to move around. It's amazing how precious seconds become as they root their classmates on. The initial times usually are about a minute and a half, with subsequent times falling below one minute. Keeping a record of scores on the board pays off. Students *ask* to review their vocabulary with this game. Roberta finds that students clamor to be chosen to play, and she allows good-natured help from classmates not holding cards.

Spending fifteen minutes preparing the cards for this game is well worth the investment. The cards can be pulled out so that the five minutes left in a class can be used constructively.

Studying the geography of Europe? Use names of countries and their capitals, exports, topography. In the midst of a poetry unit? How about the names of the poets and their poems? And, of course, every class has a vocabulary peculiar to its subject. A chance to master that vocabulary while having fun is not to be missed!

Rummy

More time-consuming but equally effective is a game Roberta uses to review reading about and charting body systems. Former student teacher Scott shared how to adapt the classic card game Rummy to a science setting, and she has used it ever since. Making the decks of cards takes a while, but laminating them makes them last a long time.

Because of the size of her classes, Roberta makes six decks of cards. Each deck is a different color so they can be separated easily; otherwise, they are alike. Each deck contains cards labeled with the names of body organs.

For those who need to review the rules of Rummy, <www.pagat.com/rummy/rummy.html> is a good source to consult before you begin. Simply adapt these rules to your own needs. To prepare students, Roberta distributes, as homework, a word bank (see Figure 7–1), which they complete using their textbook. The idea is to withdraw words from the "general fund" and "deposit" them into the proper "account." She tells them they will play a game tomorrow but no homework means no playing. (She often uses homework as a ticket to a fun activity. This is a tricky way to get them to do homework, but you only have to do it once to prove that you mean it.)

The next day, she has students count off into groups of four or five, checking to make sure that at least one person in each group has played Rummy before. She quickly explains the rules and reminds them to use their Cheat Sheets (aka word bank homework) to help them during the game. The thirty-five words in the word bank match the thirty-five cards in each deck. The object of the game is to collect seven organs in the same body system. What could be a dull listing of body parts becomes exciting as students hope for a stomach, lung, or pituitary gland on their next turn. Twenty minutes is usually enough time to play two games.

The variations here are endless: characters from the same book, countries from the same continent, math problems whose answers are the same number, words that are the same part of speech. The extra study time you gain by "letting" them use their word banks is one of those little secrets that real teachers share.

Reverse Crosswords

Crossword puzzles have been part of a teacher's repertoire for years, and the Internet's puzzle-making sites make using them even easier. For a change of pace, try *reverse crosswords* (see the example in Figure 7–2). Roberta uses them because she wants to be sure her students can express vocabulary meanings in their own words. She supplies the answers to the puzzle, and students provide the clues. Their clues can vary widely, and they enjoy sharing them with others. The conversations about their clues really help solidify their understanding of word meanings. After several practices, Roberta has even been known to give a reverse crossword as a quiz!

Riddles and Review Circles

Riddles work well as checks for comprehension. Students like to figure out ones the teacher gives and enjoy making up their own. Roberta has found them in teacher's

Science 7   Doctor _____

RUMMY (CHEAT SHEET) WORD BANK • SYSTEMS OF THE BODY

DIRECTIONS: "Withdraw" the words from the "general fund" and "deposit" them in the proper "account" below.

smooth muscle	rectum	pituitary	esophagus	nerve cell body	cerebellum
lung	ovary	right atrium	cardiac muscle	spinal cord	cerebrum
right ventricle	dendrites	thyroid	salivary glands	anus	tendon
testis	parathyroid	stomach	striated muscle	bone	medulla
left ventricle	ligament	axon	pulmonary artery	left atrium	adrenal gland
large intestine	cartilage	pancreas	pulmonary vein	small intestine	

DIGESTIVE & EXCRETORY	NERVOUS	ENDOCRINE	CARDIOPULMONARY (respiratory & circulatory)	SKELETAL & MUSCULAR

Figure 7–1. *Rummy word bank*

REVERSE CROSSWORDS

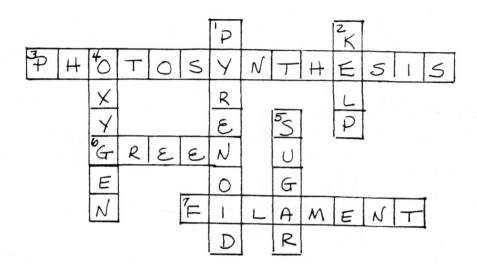

ACROSS

3.

6.

7.

DOWN

1.

2.

4.

5.

Figure 7–2.

editions of textbooks, on the Internet, and in her own creative mind. Test your science knowledge on this one that she made up:

> I am the thread of life
> Found in every cell.
> I helped Watson and Crick
> To win the prize Nobel.
> What am I?

Did you get it? The answer is *deoxyribonucleic acid*, better known as DNA. After seeing a few of these, students are more than willing to attempt their own.

Review circles (see Appendix C, pages 175–76) are variations on the riddle idea. Enter an attribute of the concept you're working on in each part of a circle (three or four parts work best). By putting the clues together, students identify *What Am I?* Sharing these the day before a test makes for a great review. When students make up their own, they automatically revisit their texts and notes. This extra visit means extra study time, and students are none the wiser!

The Yes-and-No Game

The real name is concept attainment (Joyce and Weil 1986), but students like to call it the yes-and-no game. You want your students to internalize concepts from every text they read, lecture they listen to, and video they view. Looking at exemplars (yeses) and nonexemplars (nos) strengthens their understanding of those concepts. Students think they're just playing a game, but powerful learning is taking place and higher-level thinking is rampant.

Here's how it works. Draw a T chart on the board and label the left side yes and the right side no. Write a word or phrase in the yes column that is an example of the concept you are working on; write a nonexample in the no column. Repeat with another yes, then another no, and so on until a student says he knows what the concept is. Don't let this student identify the concept; instead, have him give you another word or phrase that would fit the yes column, then a word or phrase that would fit the no column. If the student is correct, place the terms in the appropriate column and keep playing. (Tell students to see whether future additions confirm or contradict their predictions.) When most of the students are providing correct exemplars and nonexemplars, end the game by calling on someone to name the concept.

Here is a popular-culture example so you can try it for yourself:

YES	NO
Finding Forrester	The Good, the Bad, and Ugly
The Untouchables	Dances With Wolves
Raiders of the Lost Ark III	Raiders of the Lost Ark I
To Russia With Love	Live and Let Die

The concept? It's easy if you are a movie buff. The yeses are all movies starring Sean Connery, the nos are not. Now here's a history example:

YES	NO
Thomas Jefferson	Abraham Lincoln
Delegate	Candidate
Philadelphia	New York

DC museum	LA museum
Document	Song
July 4	December 7

If you figured out that all of the yeses had something to do with the Declaration of Independence, while the nos did not, you were correct. We have seen students get so caught up with the yes-and-no game that they spontaneously turn to their texts, reach for a dictionary, or pull other reference material off the shelf to clarify their thinking. In other words, it gets them to do what we want them to do without their knowing it!

Sensory Impressions: The Other Side of the Brain

Much of what we do in school is geared to the logical left side of the brain (McCarthy 1991, Jensen 1998). But the more sensory and creative right side of the brain also has a place in our academic classes. Sensory impressions can be triggered by simple sentence starters following reading, listening, or viewing:

> I saw . . .
> I heard . . .
> I touched it. It felt like . . .
> I smelled it. It smelled like . . .
> I tasted it. It tasted like . . .

Coming up with sensory impressions is a natural follow-up to talk about events in history or a piece of literature: *In the Civil War, I saw the red of blood, the blue and gray of the uniforms—tasted the salt of tears—smelled the acrid smell of gunsmoke—felt the heat of the fires.* But, don't stop there. Try it with nonevents like magnets: *I saw silver magnets and black filings—the magnets felt hard, cold—I heard the clinking of attraction—they tasted metallic and bitter.* Depending on the age of your students, you may want to eliminate "taste" if you think it would encourage real rather than imagined tasting! Some of your students will say, *What? This is dumb. You can't* touch *the Civil War."* Others, however, will hit their stride with an activity like this, showing the rest how to "think outside the box." Interestingly, many times it is the students who have the most difficulty with the logical left-brain activities who really shine in making and sharing these right-brain connections. And to that we say hurray!

Music and Multiple Intelligences

Do some research on the amount of money teenagers spend on CDs, and you'll know that music is something they value highly. As Howard Gardner (1993) has told us, everyone has multiple intelligences. Why not tap into students' interests and cultivate another of their intelligences at the same time? In her geography class, Sue challenged her students to make up their own song that listed the fifty state capitals after they had listened to "Wakko's America" (1983) from *Steven Spielberg Presents ANIMANIACS* and Rockapella singing "Capital" (1992) from *Where in the World Is Carmen San Diego?* Jim, another social studies teacher, started every class by putting a baseball cap on backwards, pulling down the world map, and leading students in raps that listed the countries found on each continent. Even University of Pennsylvania professor Helen C. Davies sets crucial information about diseases to well-known tunes to help her premed and medical students memorize information about streptococci, leprosy, and congenital infections (Kadaba 2001).

Roberta's song listing all the elements on the periodic table does not inspire new songwriters but elicits groans instead. One song that does help her students go over their reading, however, is "The Amoeba Hop," by Christine Lavin (n.d.). After receiving a copy of the lyrics, they underline the vocabulary words and circle those they can act out. While listening to the music and lyrics, both the students and Roberta are busy flapping and shaking their arms and stomping their feet to simulate the movement of amoeba hairs and splashing puddles. At the same time they are exercising still another of their intelligences, this time bodily/kinesthetic!

Roberta's students regularly summarize and demonstrate knowledge via musical and artistic renderings. After a unit on energy, Roberta challenged them to create an advertisement to promote energy conservation. Some students made posters, others created TV spots, Ashley created a radio advertisement:

[Musical interlude plays.]

Are you tired of paying hundreds of dollars to heat your home? Do you get discouraged when you pay your electric bill? Well, friends, this is your lucky day. I have just the solution for you. I can save you hundreds—yes, hundreds—of dollars. Are you interested in my secret? It's really quite simple. It's the sun! That's right. The same sun that gives you that annoying sunburn and melts your ice cream in the summer. All you have to do is buy [music starts and she sings] SUN-SHINE SO-LAR CELLS! Oh, this device works magic! It lays on your roof while semiconductors inside are busy saving you money [coins rattle in jar] by converting the sun's rays into electricity. Then this electricity is used to heat water inside your house. Now, I know what you're thinking. What's the catch? Sorry, folks, but this offer has no glitches. It's priceless. You don't have to worry if your energy source is going to run out or if the environment is suffering from something you've done. You help yourself and the earth by using [music starts and she sings] SUN-SHINE SO-LAR CELLS!

[Followed by music interlude.]

Ashley was a talented musician and to her music was a way of processing and communicating information. Her more creative right brain gave voice to her more logical left-brain knowledge. Or was it the other way around?

Venn Diagrams

She'd like to know whom to thank, but it happened so long ago that Roberta no longer remembers who introduced her to Venn diagrams. These interlocking circles have made a huge difference in her classes. She also thinks they have improved her own critical thinking skills! She uses these in many ways throughout the year, but the most common way is as a review after reading.

She introduces the idea of Venn diagrams (see example in Figure 7–3) by drawing two overlapping circles on the board and using them to compare and contrast dogs and cats. Most students in her rural area have pets and love to talk about them, so using the overlapping section to list similar attributes is easy. Then she moves to the nonoverlapping parts of the circles to list the attributes of dogs that are not common to cats and vice versa. The understanding of how Venn diagrams work is now in place, and she quickly follows with one about the most recent reading assignment. After completing this together, students are ready to complete one for homework. Depending on the ability levels of her classes, Roberta assigns a number of items that must be in each section of diagram. More able classes are assigned more items than her classes of inclusion or mainstreamed students.

Roberta's encounters with two students brought home the usefulness of Venn diagrams. Tai approached Roberta after school one day with an academic problem:

TAI: Can I talk with you a minute? You know that test we are having tomorrow?

ROBERTA: Yes.

TAI: Well, I don't understand this unit. [Roberta tries to hide her dismay. This is the last thing that any teacher wants to hear before a test. Although it's better to hear it before the test rather than after.]

ROBERTA: What don't you understand?

TAI: Everything.

ROBERTA: What do you mean, *everything*? You got good grades on your labs and reading guides. You paid attention during the review. What part of this unit don't you understand?

TAI: Everything.

ROBERTA: Let's look at how we've reviewed. We've gone over all of the conclusions for the labs. We've reviewed the reading guides and quizzes. You had a review assignment for homework and we played a vocabulary game.

TAI: But when I sit down and look at this unit, it doesn't make sense to me. [Roberta decides to focus on the labs. As she questions Tai, it becomes clear that she doesn't understand the concept of three methods of heat transfer—conduction, convection, and radiation.]

Science 8: Unit Six   Optometrist _____

VENN DIAGRAM - TYPES OF LENSES

DIRECTIONS: Use your text, notes, and labs to compare and contrast two types of lenses -
convex and concave. Include at least four items in each section.

CONVEX   CONCAVE

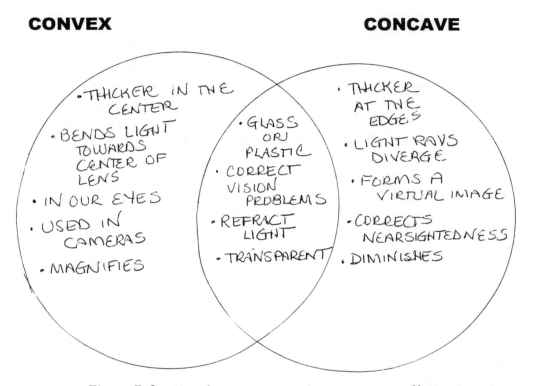

Figure 7–3. *Venn diagram to compare/contrast two types of lenses*

ROBERTA: See if this helps. [She draws three overlapping circles on the board and labels
each with a type of heat transfer. Tai quickly and easily fills them in. It is obvious
that she *did* understand the unit.]

TAI: Now everything makes sense!

Tai was able to synthesize all the information from the unit and construct a visual model
that clarified this information in an organized way.

A similar thing happened when Roberta was asked to tutor a colleague's daughter
who was having difficulty with high school biology. She worked with this student for
an evening, then asked her colleague the next morning how she thought it went:

ROBERTA: What did Robin think when she got home last night? Did she think it was time well spent? Does she feel like she understands the text now?

COLLEAGUE: I talked to her when she got home and she feels like she'll do a good job on the test now. Frankly, I looked at the notes and they make no sense to me. All of those drawings—what do you call them?

ROBERTA: Venn diagrams.

COLLEAGUE: Well, Robin assured me that they make sense to her. [Laughing] I guess I'll leave it at that!

Repeatedly, students and teachers use the phrase "make sense" to describe the benefits of organizing thinking on Venn diagrams. Roberta uses them throughout the year in different ways. Early in the year, she explains how they work and uses them as a note-taking strategy or as part of a reading guide. By the middle of the year, she includes them on quizzes, having students fill them in and then write two paragraphs, one about similarities and one about differences. By the end of the year, she asks students to write comparison and contrast paragraphs, sometimes with a hint that they might want to create a Venn diagram before writing. She delights in finding them in the margins, even when she hasn't given the hint! They are multipurpose and multi-age.

Hidden Messages: An Excuse for Friendly Nagging

Let's face it. You've got to be creative when reviewing what students have learned. If you talk too much, students tune out; if you a play game too often, it gets boring. Roberta likes to provide variety, and her students look forward to discovering the "friendly nagging" in her periodic hidden messages. "Keep an organized notebook" is the one conveyed in Figure 7–4. In order to figure it out, students have to solve the "clipped" definitions. Roberta expects her students to make the unique vocabulary of science their own. In other words, she doesn't want them to memorize definitions but to be able to explain things in their own words. The as-short-as-possible definitions she provides as clues foster understanding, not memorizing, key terms in their textbook.

Want to make a hidden message? It's simple. First decide on the message, then list as many terms as possible from a text they have read. From that list, choose words that will fit the message and create the puzzle. Sometimes Roberta offers a "free point" on the next test (or some other reward) to the first student or group to complete the hidden message. This keeps them on their toes.

Vocabulary Bingo

Most students know how to play bingo, so vocabulary bingo (Figure 7–5) captures their enthusiasm and interest. The directions are easy to understand, yet the game requires

HIDDEN MESSAGE

Directions: Use the clues to find answers. Be careful—
spelling is important! The letters in the box will give a
message!

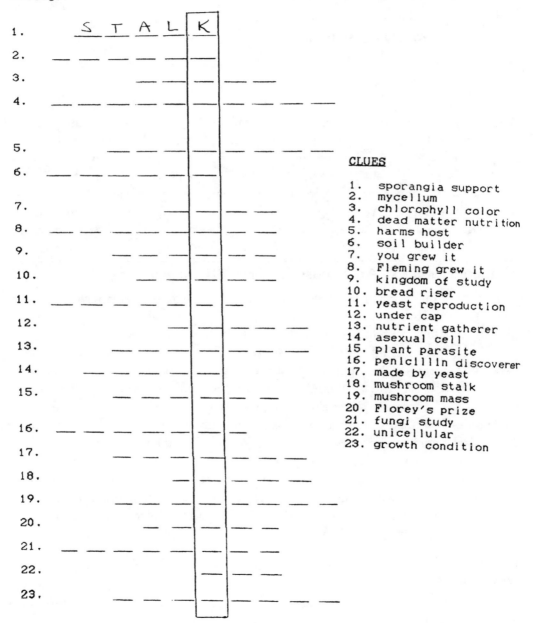

1.   S T A L K

CLUES

1.   sporangia support
2.   mycelium
3.   chlorophyll color
4.   dead matter nutrition
5.   harms host
6.   soil builder
7.   you grew it
8.   Fleming grew it
9.   kingdom of study
10. bread riser
11. yeast reproduction
12. under cap
13. nutrient gatherer
14. asexual cell
15. plant parasite
16. penicillin discoverer
17. made by yeast
18. mushroom stalk
19. mushroom mass
20. Florey's prize
21. fungi study
22. unicellular
23. growth condition

Figure 7–4.

VOCABULARY BINGO

DIRECTIONS: Use your vocabulary list, textbook, labs, and notes to find important words in this unit. Fill in the spaces below ONLY with terms that you can identify. During the game, only the definition will be read, NOT the word. Hint: Do some extra studying!

		Biology (free space)		

Figure 7–5.

that students think and study. Just what we teachers want. Because almost everybody knows how to play this game, students' mental energy can be focused on the definitions, not learning how to play the game. It makes the perfect review.

A, B, C . . . Simple! And Jigsawing

Our colleague Sue has used the alphabet to kick-start unit reviews for many years. It is an easy way to provide clues to help students as they tackle a lengthy assignment. With Sue's permission (thanks, Sue, and remember that imitation is the sincerest form of flattery), Roberta has adapted this idea to her science classes and added the cooperative learning strategy of jigsawing (see Appendix D, pages 177–80).

Take a good look at the directions. Students are divided into three different sections within the class. For homework, each student is responsible for completing only his or her section. The next day, Roberta checks for completion: the rule is, "No homework, no help," and any student not completing the homework has to do the whole thing alone. Since students love the idea of reducing their work load, most arrive in class the next day ready to consult with others to complete the form. First each student sits down with another "expert" who completed the same section to double-check each other's work. Then they regroup with an expert from each of the other two sections to teach, learn, and copy from one another. The reward for completing the assigned section is help with the other two. They get to see that the consequence of doing a good job on their homework is the opportunity to socialize while preparing themselves for a test. Student empowerment!

The Carousel Walk

Want to provide bodily/kinesthetic movement, cooperative learning, and critical thinking all at the same time? Then, the carousel walk, also known as the rotating review (Kagan 1988), is for you. Roberta has used this with eighth graders to review a chemistry unit— and also with her colleagues to review a teacher inservice meeting. Merry-go-rounds and carousels are popular carnival rides, so most students understand the concept of this activity right away. (Since these rides are much tamer than the super-duper-double-looping-scream-machines they're so drawn to, they also get the idea that they will be *walking*, not running, around a circle to complete their review!)

Ahead of time, Roberta tears sheets of rolled paper into three-to-four-foot lengths and labels the top of each one with a different concept. For her unit on chemistry, the labels are *acids, bases, solutions, suspensions, colloids, physical changes,* and *chemical changes.* Because she teaches in a typical science classroom lined with cabinets and shelves, there's not enough wall space to hang seven sheets of paper. So for this activity, her classes go across the hall to the cafeteria or sometimes out into the hallway, where there is plenty of space to hang these charts on the walls.

Before the carousel walk begins, Roberta models how the activity should proceed—just like a good coach would. On a separate long sheet of paper, she lists categories of information that would be relevant for completing these review charts: definitions, characteristics, examples, lab activities, descriptions, uses, and facts. On still another paper, using the listed categories, she talks them through preparing a review sheet for a concept from the preceding unit. (She doesn't use complete sentences, since the purpose of this activity is to jot notes quickly.)

Then the fun begins. She breaks the class into seven groups, either by counting off or by the judicious dividing and separating of certain personalities. (Such is the work of real teachers.) She gives a marker to the most "marker responsible" person in each group—one with legible handwriting who won't draw tattoos on classmates. Each group gathers around one of the sheets and begins to list as many things as they can think of about that concept. After three minutes, Roberta calls "Walk!" and each group walks, carousel-fashion, to the next sheet of paper/concept.

Roberta sits and keeps time. She approaches a group only when she sees that they are blocked for ideas or forget that it's okay to "agree to disagree." She expects them to write as much as possible and to evaluate the accuracy of the previous entries. Are the examples correct? Are all of the characteristics given? It gets harder to think of new things to write as time goes by. Questions arise about the accuracy of the listings on the sheets. Rather than giving the correct answers, Roberta lets students debate among themselves. This community-of-learners interaction and disequilibrium pique interest and involvement. After all groups have rotated past all seven sheets, the students and the sheets of paper return to the classroom where Roberta and the students evaluate, change, and clarify any misunderstandings.

On a very pragmatic note that only real teachers understand, we offer two final pieces of advice:

- Give each group a different-color marker. This will help you continue your on-going monitoring of who is weak/strong on concepts.
- Stay on the good side of your principal and custodian by placing newspaper behind your sheets of paper. No one wants this great activity to be outlawed because marker ink seeped onto the walls.

Our Questioning Nature

We can't avoid it. It seems there must be fine print in our contracts that says, *Your job is to ask students questions.* Isn't it interesting, though, that school is the only place in real life where the people who already know the answers (teachers) ask the questions? *Who was the . . . What was the . . . When was the . . . ?* Shouldn't it be the other way around? Alas, we continue to ask away. Since students learn what we value by what we do, let's make sure that the questions we ask are ones that encourage thinking and grow from authentic purposes. Dorsey Hammond (1985) suggests a framework for questioning that makes a lot of sense. If you are actively engaging students before, during, and after, these questions will follow from some genuine need to know. Here they are:

- Did we find answers to our questions? (Which ones, and what were the answers?)
- Are some of our questions still unanswered? (If so, where will we look to find the answers?)
- What else did we learn that we didn't even have questions for? (What were they? Why didn't we ask them?)
- What was the most surprising or interesting thing we learned?
- How is what we know now different from what we thought before?

This line of questioning is a good model for learning for the rest of one's life. It still gets at the content contained in the text, but it invites thinking that goes well beyond regurgitation of facts. Discussion is tied into purpose (*Did we find answers to our questions?*), further investigation (*Are some questions still unanswered?*), learning that goes beyond the expected (*What did we learn that we didn't even have questions for?*), interest (*What was the most surprising or interesting thing we learned?*), and ongoing metacognitive growth (*How is what we know now different from what we thought before?*).

The *Big* After

After you've taught a unit, put away the materials that went with it, and moved on to a new topic, don't you wonder how much of that unit has "stuck"? Are students still mindful of the content and concepts, or was it a fleeting moment of contact? Such concerns have haunted teachers for years and have given impetus to the "periodic review." Roberta tries to keep her reviews from becoming deadly by creating themes and adding humor.

Real teachers know what happens over a long holiday break. The point at which you leave your students is miles ahead of the point they're at when they return. To keep their students thinking about science over winter break, Roberta and her colleague Al give an extra-credit assignment related to the units they are teaching. Entitled The Cure for the "I Miss Science!" Blahs (see Figure 7–7), it offers students many choices that allow them to capitalize on their various strengths and interests. Seventh-grade life science students, for example, receive an extra-credit opportunity to examine holiday trees. They are to examine a live evergreen (cut, potted, or planted) and determine its type and characteristics. Not enough work to engender dread, and with just enough of a light touch, an assignment like this keeps the science wheels turning until school is in session again.

THE CURE FOR THE "I MISS SCIENCE!" BLAHS

EXTRA-CREDIT PROJECTS FOR OUR LIGHT AND SOUND UNITS

Vacation. Free time. No homework. No science labs! Help! Of course you will miss your science class over the next few days. Earn extra-credit points by completing ONE of the following projects.

Projects are due on _____

1. *Report on Isaac Newton*—Newton is famous for his work on gravity. Did you also know that he has made many important contributions to our understanding of light? Tell us all about it.

2. *Poster on an optical illusion*—Make another for us to enjoy. Posters should be neat and be at least 15 by 18 inches in size.

3. *Poster or graph of decibel levels*—Minimum size is 21 by 25 inches. Graphs and illustrations are great additions.

4. *Large timeline of the technological history of sound recordings.*

5. *Flip Book*—Make at least 20 drawings using the same techniques employed in animation for cartoons. The drawings are to be neat and stapled together. Make the paper a three-inch square. Use science ideas (lenses, rockets, reactions, etc.). Use your imagination. You may join with friends to present your story in longer form but each person is responsible for creating his/her own flip book.

6. *Diagram on the construction of the ruby-red laser*—Label all parts! Must be at least 16 by 20 inches.

7. *Poster showing how sound travels from one person to another*—Minimum size is 21 by 25 inches.

8. *Poster showing the different types of sound waves*—(high and low pitch, loud and soft sounds). Be sure to label all parts. Minimum size is again 21 by 25 inches.

9. *Poster of the human eye*—be sure to label all parts. Minimum size is 21 by 25 inches.

10. *Periscope*—Use a shoebox and two pocket mirrors. Tape the mirrors facing each other at 45-degree angles at opposite ends of the box. Cut a window opposite each mirror and then put the cover on with tape.

These and other ideas are related to our light and sound units. Be neat. Have fun!

Figure 7–6.

Since science-related stories are always in the news, Roberta and her students regularly clip them out and bring them to class. In the past, Roberta filed them away so she could refresh her memory about them later if she needed to. Once, years after the Three Mile Island nuclear power incident, she was talking about it with her classes when she realized that she couldn't remember all the surrounding circumstances. If *she* couldn't remember something of this magnitude that she had lived through, and *she* was the science teacher, how could she expect her students to remember current events in their lives? Since that time, whenever a significant science development or event occurs, she has volunteers take all of the clipped articles and pictures relating to the incident and arrange them artfully on a poster. Once laminated, these posters hang in Roberta's classroom to remind her students of the events that have touched their lives that year. As an added bonus, Roberta has a nice collection of visuals to use with future classes.

By far the most-looked-forward-to event of the year (other than the last day) in Roberta's classes is the annual Super Bowl of Science. This semester review coincides with the NFL's yearly contest and all its hype. Joining in the fun, Roberta uses a poster to announce the scholastic gridiron contest. She tells students to dress in the colors of their favorite team in that year's Super Bowl and to bring in pennants and posters proclaiming their team allegiance. Students choose teams based on their NFL preference. Does anyone doubt that middle schoolers can be vocal and opinionated? Get them talking about sports teams and watch their volume and enthusiasm rise! Non–sports fans even out the number of players on each team, and get just as caught up in the action.

On game day, the Friday before the professional game, Roberta dresses in a referee's uniform, complete with whistle. The overhead projector beams an aerial view of a football field onto the screen at the front of the classroom. A toss-up question gives possession of the ball, a cardboard cutout, to one team. Roberta reads from a script of questions that cover everything from the first day of school on; therefore, if a student gets a tough one, it's just bad luck; Roberta can't be accused of setting up one team to lose. Teams advance ten yards with each correct answer. Incorrect answers result in fumbles recovered by the opposing team. Field goals may be kicked from the twenty-yard line (they're successful if another question is answered). Touchdowns result in hooting and hollering, so she makes sure to remind her principal ahead of time so he knows that it's Super Bowl day, not Donnybrook Fair, in room 22!

Each class's score is posted on the board. You might be surprised by the seriousness with which these students approach an answer when it is their turn. Heavy thinking goes on as they search their brains for information covered months ago. Roberta reminds each class to listen for the combined results of the games during end-of-the-day announcements. Not only the students, but faculty, former students, parents, and even community members anxiously await the results of the Super Bowl of Science each year. Why? Because, for a ten-year period, the winning team in the Super Bowl of Science has *lost* the real game two days later. While Roberta appreciates the excitement generated by the Super Bowl of Science, she hopes no one ever places bets based on her game!

Aftermath

The *after* part of reading can be like pulling teeth. We know; we've done it that way. We reiterate that *after* reading, listening, or lecture can be fun, but *only if* the *before* and *during* phases are done well. BDA activities should involve students actively and socially while they learn. With adolescents, particularly, socialization is one of their reasons for coming to school. (And anyone who has taught for more than twenty minutes can tell you that "inactive learning" is an oxymoron.)

So, have fun teaching BDA. We sense your anxiety—*If I do these things, will I still have enough time to cover my content?* If you remember, we questioned this in the beginning, too. We now know that Roberta has been able not only to cover her content but also to go further and deeper into it. Even more important, her students become better scientists *and better readers.*

CHAPTER 8

SELLING READING: CREATING A LIFETIME HABIT

Selling reading? That can't be *my* job!

Oh, yes, it can. "Selling" reading as a viable lifetime habit is every educator's shared accountability. Here's why. Research in *emergent literacy* (Clay 1967, 1991; Holdaway 1979; Teale and Sulzby 1989) has examined the environmental conditions surrounding young children who emerge naturally as readers and writers. Children who emerge early and successfully as readers and writers in school tend to come from homes in which *school-like* literacy is valued and practiced. They have seen the significant adults in their lives reading and writing, have been read to and talked with about books, and have had access to a print-rich environment of books, paper, markers, and other literacy tools.

What does this mean for real teachers? Simply that the students of today will be the parents of tomorrow. If we fail to create in them the lifelong habit of reading and writing, they will not instill the value of—and provide the all-important model of—reading and writing in and for their children. Those children, in turn, will find it difficult to learn to read and write and, in turn, will not value or model these processes in and for *their* children—and the cycle of *aliteracy, marginal literacy,* and *illiteracy* will continue. We, as educators, must join hands to share the accountability across grades and subjects to send students into the world at the end of grade 12 who are firmly steeped in the love and habits of literacy. We have much to lose if we don't.

So, how do real teachers do this? Here are two guiding points:

- *Be a reader.*
- *Create a community-of-readers ethos in your classroom and school.*

Be a Reader

Take the following quiz—and *be honest*.

AM I A MODEL OF A "READER"?

Can I describe three books that I have read in the past year?	Yes	No
Do I read a newspaper every day?	Yes	No
Do I subscribe to and read magazines?	Yes	No
Do I talk with others about what I currently am reading?	Yes	No
Do I own and use a library card?	Yes	No
Proportionately, do I spend about as much time reading as I do watching TV and videos?	Yes	No
Do I spend time browsing in bookstores in malls?	Yes	No
Do I give books and magazine subscriptions as gifts?	Yes	No
Do others (particularly young people) see me reading?	Yes	No
Can I name three books on my "waiting list" of books I intend to read next?	Yes	No
Do I have a favorite author?	Yes	No
Can I name three books currently on the bestseller list?	Yes	No
Do I ask others (particularly young people), What are you reading?	Yes	No
Do I take along something to read in case I'm kept waiting?	Yes	No

How did you do? Probably most of us don't score 100 percent. Our point is not to compare scores but to get all of us to reflect on our own literacy practices. How would your community respond to this quiz? What would happen if we substituted *view* for *read*, and *TV and videos* for *books, magazines, and newspapers*? (*Can I describe three videos I have watched in the last year? Do I watch a TV show every day? Do I own and use a video store card? Do others (particularly young people) see me watching TV?*) If it weren't so sad, it would be funny.

We have heard good and caring teachers say, *Boy, I just don't like to read; I don't read much*; or *Read? I read kid's papers all day*. On the one hand, we understand this— real teachers must deal with enormous amounts of paperwork, graduate school course-work, and the like that encroach upon reading for pleasure (and often on the more basic pleasures of sleeping and eating, as well). However, if we—the educated and the educators—do not read (or to use a much more pejorative term, are aliterate), how can we expect the rest of society to read?

We must *be* readers, and share this fact with our students and the rest of the world. Few models of literacy exist in this culture and time. Because of compulsory education in our country, we have, as captive audiences for thirteen years, *all of the people* at very impressionable times of their lives. What we model for them during that time is profound and lasting. We truly do not know how far our influence reaches. What we share of ourselves is "glue" that will stick to our students long after they forget that we taught them the Pythagorean Theorem, the parts of government, or the speed of sound.

Here is just one story to prove it. Terry was a first grader in Donna's class. Periodically, Donna's father would stop by her classroom. Terry delighted in greeting and talking to him in grown-up, "man-to-man" fashion. Ten years later Donna encountered "little" Terry, now six feet tall, in the high school corridor. He immediately asked her how her father was. She was surprised that Terry still remembered but even more staggered by his next question: "Does he still like to read those spy stories?" Donna has no memory of telling her first graders about her father's reading preferences. But apparently she had. And, ten years later, this young man still had a strong association between an adult he had admired and a model of literacy. The glue sticks. We have an opportunity to make a real difference, if we dare to share ourselves as readers. Students expect their reading specialists, librarians, and English teachers to talk about books and care about reading. It's another thing entirely when the physical education, math, industrial arts, and history teachers model reading as well.

What constitutes a model? A full-period book talk once a week? Not necessarily. Simple things are quite effective. Several images come to mind in connection with some of our colleagues. We see Steve, a trig teacher, walking down the hall with the *Philadelphia Inquirer* tucked on top of his gradebook and textbook. Students know he's a reader. We see Becky, the English teacher, whose stack of teaching materials is always topped with the novel she currently is reading for pleasure. They know what she values in her personal life. We hear casual comments like these: Hey, did ya see the article in *Sports Illustrated* on thus-and so? Boy, am I tired today—stayed up last night to finish reading [name of book]. I was at one of those parts where I just couldn't put it down until I found out, so have mercy because I'm paying for it today! I just love/hate stories that do such-and-such. We read about a physical education teacher in Kansas who brings in his old issues of *Sports Illustrated, Sport Magazine,* and *Soccer America* and places them in a Read-and-Return Box (Idea Exchange 1992). Our students will know we're readers by what we show, tell, and encourage.

Roberta makes a point to do this in her classes. Think back to our SQ3R example: you probably noticed how freely she shares herself as a reader, not by lecture or book review, but by casually weaving her reading habit into the fabric of her lesson. Her nightmares triggered by reading Stephen King, her favorite authors, and the book she'll continue reading that night are mentioned within the context of what she intends to teach. Her students know that she reads.

The Community-of-Readers Ethos

We need to establish a *community-of-readers ethos* in our schools and communities. We're alive, we breathe, we read. It's as natural as that. We laugh, albeit sardonically, at the story of the elementary teacher who showed her youngsters the signs for *greater than* and *less than* (> and <), only to find that they called them "fast forward" and "rewind"! A number of years ago, our state distributed to each school district a box of bumper stickers, bookmarks, and posters that encouraged people to ask children what they were currently reading. This minicampaign was an attempt to encourage our state's residents to engage as a community of readers with our youth. The campaign was short-lived and was replaced all too soon by a twelve-million-dollar state testing program, and we have to wonder what would have happened if that twelve million dollars had been spent on raising public awareness about literacy, putting books into schoolrooms and citizens' hands.

So much for complaining about what we cannot control. What can we *do*, as real teachers, to create this community of readers in our classrooms and schools? Roberta's classroom proclaims "Read me!" In a very traditional secondary science room of lab tables and equipment closets, a number of atypical things are evident. Bright posters filled with newspaper and magazine articles and pictures related to the current unit of study invite a reader's attention. An accessible table just inside the door is filled with pamphlets; brochures; copies of *Life, Time, National Geographic World,* and *Science World*; and newspaper articles, all dealing with science topics. And occupying a place of honor beside her teacher's lab table is *the cart.*

The Cart

The cart, itself, is unremarkable. Left over from a previous life in the library, its four shelves are loaded with science-related books. Note that we didn't say science *text*-books. These are books culled from yard sales, used-book sales, sale tables at bookstores, the school library, and the generous donations of Roberta and others. In her classroom, Roberta makes book club order forms, traditionally the province of language arts teachers only, available and uses the bonus points to order free books for the cart. Because her school district's budget for science is to be used for lab supplies and equipment, there is no money for purchasing books. So when she buys cart books, she claims them as income tax deductions. (A fortunate colleague from another district was given a check for a thousand dollars and told to go purchase books for his social studies classroom!)

Titles range from *102 Creepy, Crawly Bug Jokes* (Michaels 1992) and *Blood and Guts: A Working Guide to Your Own Insides* (Allison 1976) to biographies of Madame Curie. Roberta shops for books that will grab students' attention, without regard for grade levels. In a mall science store one summer, she asked a salesperson to help her find a certain book. Because of the title he immediately assumed she was an elementary school teacher. When she told him she was purchasing it for seventh graders, he scoffed and put it down. He, too, taught middle school and felt that the book was more appropriate for fourth and fifth graders. Roberta disagreed. This book, like others in its series, had beautiful and interesting photographs that she knew would draw in her students. Especially for reluctant readers or those having difficulty reading, an unopened book is an unread book. If the pictures lure them in and the reading level is comfortable, they will *read science*. That is the purpose of the cart.

Students have checked out the copy of *The After-Dinner Gardening Book* (Langer 1969) so many times that it now is held together by rubber bands. The books with the largest circulation by far are those containing images from electron microscopes. These photomicrographs open up a new world to students—the bumps and ridges on pins, the roughness of razor blades, the complexity of hair, the similarity between snake fangs and hypodermic needles, and the grossness of human scalps and tongues when seen up close and personal. The demand for these books is so high that Roberta, having paid to buy them and then (after hard use) rebind them, has had to restrict them to the classroom.

Multiple copies of *Hiroshima* (Hersey 1985) also circulate each year. Roberta features it in a quick sales pitch by telling a bit of one of the survivors' stories at the beginning of class. She also mentions that she was greatly moved by an article she had read in a magazine about a thirteen-year-old boy (her students' age) who was seated in his first-period class in the row by the window when the bomb exploded. (Of course, everyone always turns and stares at the student in that seat in her class.) The boy in the article was the only one in his school who survived the blast; he was thrown out the window just before the building collapsed on everyone else. Invariably, students ask for a copy of the article to read. For many years, she had to tell them that she no longer had a copy of the magazine. Then she had Miguel in her class. He was so interested in the story that he went to the local university and located and photocopied the article. It circulated among the students for two months. Roberta kept track: eighteen out of the twenty-two students in that class read this twenty-page article—*without* being assigned it and without receiving any points toward their grades. When teachers find the "hook" (in this case, the similarity of ages), students will read.

Donna's daughter, Allyson, brought home a copy of *Hiroshima* from Roberta's science class one day, eager to share this exciting new find with her family. (Never mind that two copies of this book had sat on the family bookshelves for years. *Mrs. McManus*, not Mom, had recommended it, so it had to be good.) She devoured it in an evening. Another student, Katy, returned to class the day after checking it out and said to the class, "I'm almost done. You know, this is the kind of book that, once you get started, you just can't put it down."

Appendix E contains Roberta's students' current list of favorites. What is remarkable is the amount of reading for pleasure that these books inspire. Roberta typically starts each unit with a brief "sales pitch" for one or two of these books by reading aloud an excerpt or a joke or showing photos or illustrations from it.

That's it. That's all it takes. A couple of books "sold" each day, and the cart becomes a circulating science library. Students sign these books out by filling in their name, the date, and the name of the book in a simple notebook. When they're finished, they cross out their entries. Roberta has tracked the cart's circulation rate and found that she typically circulates in excess of ninety science-related books per month by the last months of school each year. (How many science-related books circulate from most middle school libraries each month?) Because the local high school is just next door, her former students often walk over to her classroom to borrow books that they remember from science class. The personal touch of the teacher's enthusiasm makes all the difference.

Science purists may shudder and the literati may swoon at some of the books on the cart, but they cannot deny that Roberta gets students into the habit of reading for pleasure. The titles all may not be highfalutin, but the books lure them into reading about science—and into reading period. During adolescence, many things compete with reading for students' attention; studies have shown that the higher the grade level, the more infrequently they read (Wiscont 1990). Neither scientific nor literary tastes can be developed if students are not reading at all. Light reading like this whets the appetite; gourmet tastes can be developed and refined in time.

SSR: Sit Down and What?

Roberta asked her nephew about the sustained silent reading (SSR) program in his school. He said, "SSR? You know what that means? Sit down. Shut up. And read."

How sad. SSR, when done well, not only has enormous potential to help us establish a community of readers in our schools, but it has the consistent effect of improving students' overall reading abilities (Pilgreen 2000, Krashen 1999). Simply stated, the more you read, the better you get at it. The practice element is strong and circular. Take Donna and sewing, for example. She doesn't sew well, so she doesn't spend her free time sewing. (She even sold her sewing machine at a yard sale for five dollars. Yes, it's that bad.) Because she doesn't practice sewing, she doesn't get better at it. Because she doesn't get better, she avoids it all the more—and so forth.

Over the years, a number of researchers and practitioners have urged teachers to include sustained silent reading activities in their classrooms (Hunt 1967, Fader and McNeil 1968, McCracken and McCracken 1972, Allington 1975, Smith 1988, Allen 1995, and others). Called by many names (uninterrupted sustained silent reading, drop everything and read, sustained quiet reading time, to name a few), it is always associated with counterbalancing skill-and-drill instruction by providing an opportunity within the school day for students to read uninterruptedly for a period of time. Students learn what we value by what we do in schools. If all we do is skill and drill, they learn that literacy is filling in worksheets and parroting answers. If we value personal reading in schools, they learn that *that* is an important part of literacy.

SSR programs are not without their problems, however. Donna regularly talks to her undergraduate teachers-to-be about their memories of SSR. Many echo the disdain expressed by Roberta's nephew. They describe environments in which SSR was about as appealing as holding your nose while you ate your brussels sprouts and took your vitamin: do it because you have to, it's good for you. (In other words, *sit down, shut up, and read.*) They remember teachers grading papers or talking to colleagues in the hall instead of modeling reading. They recall not having interesting reading materials available or being told to read their textbooks during SSR. They say they dreaded the book reports or summaries they had to create about what they had read. They describe their strategies for clock watching until it was time to get back to real school.

After surveying thirty-two studies of self-selected sustained silent reading programs, Janice Pilgreen (2000) enumerates eight factors that successful programs incorporate:

1. *Access to a "flood"* of trade books, magazines, comics, newspapers, and other reading material in the classroom, rather than relying on students to bring something to read from home.

2. *Appealing materials*, interesting and provocative enough for students to choose to read.

3. *Conducive environments* in which readers can feel comfortable and undistracted while they are reading.

4. *Encouragement* to read by seeing the teacher reading and hearing conversations among the teacher and other students about the good parts of things they are reading.

5. *Staff training* in which teachers discuss the why and how-to of SSR and discover strategies for matching readers to texts.

6. *Nonaccountability*, to underscore the pleasure aspect of personal reading: no book reports, quizzes, or traditional school-type assignments.

7. *Follow-up activities* focused on book sharing and conversations about books.

8. Reading periods that are *often enough and long enough* to make reading "habit-forming."

Spearheaded by the language arts teachers, the faculty in Roberta's school met and decided that the basic premises of SSR were valid. And it seems to be working. This middle school operates on a fairly traditional schedule of eight periods a day. Within that structure, one day each week during "club period," students join with teachers and staff in small groups of ten to fourteen for SSR. They enjoy and look forward to it. Students read for thirty minutes, then respond in their journals to what they have read. The emphasis is on *response* rather than *report*. Each marking period students create two "non–book report" projects, sharing books they have read.

This school has incorporated SSR in some version for over twenty years. During that time, Roberta has seen numerous benefits accrue to both students and staff. A particular memory stands out. Debby, not known to be a strong reader, was a student in Roberta's homeroom. At that time, homeroom, first thing in the morning, was SSR time.

Debby became hooked on romance novels; Roberta was equally enthralled with mysteries. Each day when the intercom announced that SSR was over, they both groaned. In time, they developed the kinship of readers, talking often about their respective books and what was happening at the point when they were so rudely interrupted.

Segue to an overly warm day in the spring of the year. It was only 7:45 A.M. and already tempers and hormones in this middle school were running as high as the temperature. Roberta heard a fight outside her classroom door. She went into the hall and saw Debby pulling hair, clawing, and screaming at another girl. Roberta summoned her best teacher stare and said, *"Get to your homerooms."* Debby looked at Roberta, stopped fighting, and walked into homeroom, while the other girl continued to protest. In homeroom, the other students challenged Debby. "Why did you stop fighting her? She deserved it!" Debby looked at Roberta and said, "'Cuz she's my friend; we talk about books." To this day, Roberta and Debby continue to talk about books whenever they bump into each other in town.

DIRT

Walk into Roberta's classroom any day of the week and you will find DIRT on the chalkboard. In addition to schoolwide SSR, Roberta incorporates daily independent reading time (DIRT) into her classes. Just as in your classroom, her students work at different rates. In the early years of her teaching, Roberta tried many things to fill the space between the first and last students' finishing an activity. Much of the time, she did little more than give busywork to the early finishers. The reward for completing their work efficiently was *more* work. Having reconceptualized her classes as communities of readers, she now tells her students that she will not punish them with more work for completing their science assignments. When they are finished, it's DIRT time. It goes on the board as part of the daily agenda for class. What do they read? Anything.

In the middle of a class discussion about oil-based energy one day, Kyle got out of his seat and walked over to a shelf. He rummaged through a collection of magazines until he located the copy of *Reader's Digest* he needed. He waited until Roberta got to the end of a sentence, then said, "I'd like to read this to everyone." Class discussion had reminded him of an article he had read during DIRT. He transfixed the class for the next several minutes as he read to them about Red Adair, the world famous "go-to" person for putting out oil-well fires, whose credit card melted to his shirt from the heat of an oil fire.

Never Too Late for Reading Aloud

The *science* teacher reads aloud to her students? How can she justify taking time away from the curriculum when she has so much to cover? Anyway, isn't read-aloud just for little kids? We respond in the words of Jim Trelease, author of multiple editions of *The Read-Aloud Handbook* (1995), "Far from suggesting the curriculum be abandoned, [we] say it should be enriched and brought to life by story (1989, 37)." Roberta reads to her middle schoolers. Both Donna and principal-turned-college-professor Ken read aloud to their university students (the people stories of education are compelling). Reading aloud knows no age boundaries. As Ken says, "I don't care how old kids are, they still like to be read to."

Roberta's students quickly become accustomed to hearing her read aloud for sustained periods. It all begins when she writes the word *serendipity* on the chalkboard at the beginning of the year. Students have fun rolling this word around in their mouths, but usually there is only one who has ever heard it before. Ceremoniously, then, Roberta goes to the dictionary, looks it up, and reads it aloud. Building on the idea of "lucky accidents," she introduces her first read-aloud, *Serendipity: Accidental Discoveries in Science* (Roberts 1989). Delightedly, they hear about the discovery of penicillin, the first successful vaccination, and the work of Madame Curie.

The serendipity theme continues throughout the year. To introduce her lessons on Lyme disease, Roberta reads aloud from *Medical Mysteries: Six Deadly Cases* (Buchman 1992). She opens six days of class by reading three pages from this easy-to-understand book. Most students (and adults, we suspect) are totally unfamiliar with the role two concerned mothers played in bringing this disease to the attention of the medical community. Serendipity appears more than once in this compelling story. These women, who did not know each other, each kept records of the high incidence of illness in Lyme, Connecticut. They just happened to call the state health department at the same time to report their findings. They just happened to talk to the same man, who just happened to have been trained by the Center for Disease Control and Prevention. He just happened to put the pieces of information together, and thus the medical community began the search that led to deer ticks. Roberta also likes to read aloud sections of Edwin Kiester, Jr.'s article "A Curiosity Turned into the First Silver Bullet Against Death," from *Smithsonian* (November 1990). Stories of wartime precautions, deadly strep throat, and doctors who were not sure how—or *whether*—to administer this new thing called *penicillin* capture students' attention. They gladly listen and ask for more.

Roberta finds that short read-alouds are also big hits in her classes. She introduces a lab in which students use mirrors to study the reflection of light rays by reading Panati's (1987) story about the origin of the relationship between seven years of bad luck and broken mirrors; it's a wonderful way to remind students to be careful handling their lab equipment. Another story from this book brings a lesson in which she uses a Slinky™ to demonstrate sound waves. The creator of this familiar childhood toy "invented" it when he was trying to make an antivibration instrument for use on ships.

Do you know that the largest seaweed can grow eighteen inches a day? Or that the world's largest fungus covers fifteen hundred acres in the state of Washington? The *Guinness Book of World Records* (Guinness Publishing 1999) tempts students with assorted curricularly related facts, is an often-requested read-aloud, and fits in well when there is a minute here and a minute there.

Old books make for interesting read-aloud tie-ins to the curriculum. Roberta's students had just completed a reading guide in which they had developed a timeline with dates, explanations, and drawings of the different stages of human knowledge about the development of atomic theory. The next day a student brought in an old encyclopedia that her parents had found at a yard sale. Without revealing the date of the book, Roberta quickly read aloud a section, stating with certainty that scientists now know that electrons, and electrons only, constitute what they know as matter. Amid laughter, students consulted their charts and placed this 1911 passage accurately on the timelines they had just made. For days after that, they kept wanting to look up topics in the old encyclopedia just to see how much laughter they could produce!

Roberta's school has two programs that bring faculty and students together in arrangements other than typical classes. In one, faculty and staff "advisers" meet with small groups of student "advisees" to forge more personal bonds and to discuss issues about growing up. In another, teams of students and their teachers explore a theme in an interdisciplinary way. You probably have already guessed that Roberta often spends time in these programs reading aloud. Some favorites are "Yes, Virginia, There Is a Santa Claus" (Church 1897), Martin Luther King's "I Have a Dream" speech (in Cohn 1993), and *Aesop's Fables* (translated by Temple and Temple 1998). She also reads excerpts from articles that speak not only of the athletic prowess of sports stars such as Tiger Woods, Wayne Gretzky, and Grant Hill, but also of their sportsmanship and gentlemanly manners. Before standardized tests are going to be administered, when other teachers are busy exhorting their students to eat a good breakfast in order to do their best thinking and perform at their peak, she reads aloud from her grandmother's 1918 cookbook. This treasure identifies a good breakfast as one with enough food to feed an entire contemporary family for a whole day. In addition, according to this book a meal of toast, eggs, meat, fruit, milk, cooked cereal, and more should cost the typical cook no more than eight cents per person (a frugal cook could do it for seven!). Students enjoy these incongruities but remember the point that good breakfasts are important on test day.

Read-alouds fit well into the intent of these special times between students and a trusted adult. Just as the bond between a small child and a parent is forged by the rhythm, lyricism, and rhyme of stories read aloud, so it is with students at this turbulent age. When baseball is a team theme, Roberta shares a recording of James Earl Jones reading *Casey at the Bat*, Abbott and Costello's routine *Who's on First?* (both from *Play Ball!* 1998), and the story of Jackie Robinson. She also gives them the lyrics to "Take Me Out to the Ball Game" (in Cohn 1993) and invites them to sing along. Most of Roberta's students stopped hearing a parent read to them years ago; many never experienced it at all. When she reads, a hush settles over them.

Read-aloud possibilities are endless, and we're sure you can think of logical connections to your curriculum. *From Sea to Shining Sea: A Treasury of American Folklore and Folk Songs* (Cohn 1993), with its wonderful illustrations by Caldecott Award–winning illustrators, and the Website <www.rogertaylor.com> are particularly useful sources of cross-curricular connections. If you're not sure about the possibilities, ask your colleagues or the school librarian, go browsing through bookstores, and start reading magazines and newspapers with an eye for sharing with your students.

Bring It In, Share It, Talk About It—But Be Ready for Surprises!

Roberta capitalizes on every opportunity to include real-world reading in her classes, viewing everything she reads with an eye toward sharing it with her students. A daily metropolitan newspaper sits atop the computer. She frequently reads relevant news articles aloud to her students and invites them to browse through it at the beginning and end of class. The press is a rich source of science-related coverage. The Exxon Valdez, Three Mile Island, and Chernobyl incidents all conveniently occurred during her energy unit. Mad cow, foot-and-mouth, and Lyme diseases serendipitously appeared in the press during her disease unit. (Her colleagues are thinking of asking her not to teach energy and disease any more.)

With modeling like this students begin reading the newspaper and searching the Internet for science-related articles that they clip and bring in to share with the class. It is common to hear students say, *Hey, did you hear about such-and-such on the news this morning?*, and see class members scurry to the newspaper to track down the printed story. This is not a current events *assignment*; it is a natural outgrowth of the ethos of a classroom in which the teacher reads aloud. The students are becoming *lifetime* readers, not just *schooltime* readers, as Trelease would say (1985, 71). Their "inquiring minds" really do want to know.

In real classrooms like these almost anything can happen:

• One day Cinda pulled a newspaper from her bookbag. The picture on the front page showed a woman holding a toaster under one arm and the plug in her other hand. This woman had so much electricity in her body she never had to plug the toaster in to make her children's breakfast toast! (You surely have guessed that the paper was a sensational tabloid.) After gulping, Roberta used this as an opportunity to teach about reliability of print sources.

• Roberta uses everyday products to tie science to daily life. During a chemistry unit she has her students examine product labels to determine the chemical content of their diets. It is common to find them poring over potato chip bags, milk cartons, and candy bar wrappers. They become so accustomed to reading their environments that their spontaneous remarks sometimes hold surprises. While talking about smoking, Roberta mentioned the changes in intensity over the years of the Surgeon Generals' warnings on cigarette packages, from "may be" to "is" hazardous to your health. One young lady, caught up in actively constructing meaning, reached into her purse and pulled out her own pack of cigarettes (an illegal substance in this school) to check, and said, "Well, I'll be darned. You're right!"

- Another of Roberta's students was the daughter of an artist. After a presentation on optical illusions, she brought in her father's book on M. C. Escher's tessellations. (For the uninitiated, tessellations are repeating patterns.) Students crowded around Roberta's desk to look at the pictures. Roberta turned a page, then quickly turned another. One of the students said, "Awwwwwww—I saw what you're trying to hide from us!" Roberta had just discovered that M. C. Escher was able to create optical illusions using certain male body parts!

It is never dull in Roberta's science class! The community-of-readers ethos is reminiscent of the grand conversations about which Nancie Atwell (1987, 1998) writes. Science and literacy are alive and real in the fabric of daily life and beyond. Occasionally, a high school student will return and ask, *Do you remember the time you read so-and-so to us? Do you still have that book? Could I use it again?* We were reminded of how much influence we have as teachers when Roberta received this note from Kim, whom she had taught the previous year:

> *Dear Mrs. McManus,*
>
> *I just found this article in one of my mom's magazines and thought you might like to read it. Your energy class unit really pushed me to look for this kind of material—anywhere I can. Thanx [sic] for the info you gave us. It's really helping me a lot. Now I try whatever I can to conserve energy, water, and natural resources without doing anything drastic. Thanks again—*
>
> *Sincerely yours*
>
> *Kim*
>
> *P.S. I know I don't write letters that well and I hope you can read this. (HA HA)*

Not only did Kim write the letter and include the magazine article, but she also highlighted key parts of it in yellow—another skill she had learned in science class!

We Are the Giants

Albert Einstein once noted that he was able to see so far because he had stood on the shoulders of giants. Real teachers, *we* are the giants upon whose shoulders our students stand. We calculate that by the time a student graduates from high school, about fifty teachers have spread their influence on her or him. If each of us takes the time to present ourselves as readers and to establish overt communities of readers in each of our classrooms, we can have an incredible impact on literacy!

CHAPTER 9

Slipping Writing Into the Content Area

Donna remembers how Roberta dragged her feet about incorporating writing into her classes. She jumped at ideas about reading, encouraging the habit of reading, helping students take notes and study, and wanted more, more, more! But every time Donna wanted to talk about ways to get students to write more, Roberta changed the subject. All she could think of was higher piles of papers to grade, having to bone up on grammar and mechanics before she could accurately wield her red pen, and yawn-inducing essays arriving 130 at a time. Perhaps you know the feeling.

What do you do when you write? What's it like for you? When you're faced with having to write something, do you say *Lucky me! I get to write!* Or does a dark cloud move in, blocking the sun, until the piece of writing is done and you can get rid of it? Donna has asked hundreds of students in her undergraduate and graduate classes to write their responses to these questions. They usually wince.

So stop for a minute and write about what your processes of writing are like.

What did you write? One of the funniest responses, and one that resonated with a class full of graduate students, came from an experienced teacher who put down something like this:

> When faced with the task of writing, I immediately think of all the other things I need to do. Like clean the attic. Oh, and the basement, too, because it's really dirty. Then I remember that root canal surgery I've been putting off. I call the dentist. Of course, I can't write while I'm waiting for the appointment because I'm too nervous. Then certainly I can't write after the surgery, because I need to recuperate with lots of rest. Then I decide to make a list of all the animals Noah took onto the ark. Of course, I have to copy it over because they went two by two. . . .

The list of kinds of avoidance behavior went on and on. Donna wishes that she could remember who this reluctant writer was and had asked for a copy of this piece, because it is clearly—and ironically—well written for the audience and purpose! The person who said she hated to write, had nothing to say, and avoided it at all costs penned this wonderful piece in a few minutes and then basked in the appreciation of a room full of peers. Yet she, like Roberta, preferred to avoid writing at all costs.

Understanding Writing

By the way, did you *really* write anything, or did you just keep reading? (We suspect that you kept reading.) If you are like many, your aversion to writing may have kept you from investigating it fully enough to understand it. Donna found that her own writing, and her ability to teach it, improved by learning more about the nature of it. And for two long years, she nudged (pushed, actually) Roberta with her pearls of wisdom.

A Most Natural Urge

The urge to write is more natural than the urge to read. We sense your disbelief. You're thinking, *Wait a minute—it's Sunday afternoon and I can either read the Sunday paper or a good book, or I can write. It's no contest—reading wins.* But think about it. Writing must be the more natural urge. If human beings had not had the urge to write—to take ideas and put them down for others to see—we would never have had the need to read. Long, long ago, before there was alphabetic language as we know it today, people used pictures to share their thoughts about good places to hunt, significant events that had happened, and dangers that lay in wait.

If you ask a group of kindergartners on the first day of school *How many of you can read?* very few of them raise their hands. If you ask the same group *How many of you can write?* hands shoot into the air. They come to school thinking they can write because *they have been writing* for as long as they can remember. From the time children have enough motor control to pick up something that will make a mark, they begin leaving messages for others to see. Now we all know that the marker is usually something permanent like lipstick or indelible ink and the surface is usually the wallpaper or the best tablecloth in the house. But the point is, they believe the marks they put down express their thoughts. And they bring them to us: *Look, Mommy, I'm writing a letter to Santa,* or *I'm writing my name.* We, in turn, look at these stray marks that usually resemble no letter in any language we've ever seen, and say: *Oh, what a nice list,* or *Aren't you so smart!* Rarely do we hear adults saying to these novices, *What are you—nuts? Santa's never going to be able to read those scribbles,* or *That's not real writing,* or *AWK—run-on—frag—grade = F—you can do better!*

Children come to school believing they can write and eager to do it. Somehow we turn that around during the thirteen years we have them in school and convince them that writing is worse than dental surgery. Certainly, no curriculum states *Teach them to write poorly and to hate it*, but our misunderstanding of writing and how to teach it has created this anomaly. For one thing, we don't let them write enough. Simply stated, to write better, you have to write more. Donald Graves's seminal report for the Ford Foundation entitled *Balance the Basics: Let Them Write* (1978) and numerous investigations since (Graves 1983; Atwell 1987, 1998; Murray 1989; Calkins and Harwayne 1991; Harwayne 1992; Calkins 1994; Routman 2000; McCarrier et al. 2000, Tsujimoto 2001, among others) have documented classroom practices that get students to write well. They all point to *time*: time spent writing. Writers improve their writing with instruction *about* writing, but they have to be *engaged in* writing regularly in order for that instruction to stick. Imagine trying to play the piano well by hearing someone lecture about piano playing and completing worksheets about correct piano technique but only getting to place your hands on the keyboard occasionally. Time working at the craft is as necessary for writing as it is piano playing.

Processes in Motion

We have to let students write. By this we mean giving them frequent and regular opportunities to write—for a variety of purposes—every day—all day long. Before you throw down this book, having decided we are not *real* teachers after all because we don't understand what it's like to face mountains of papers to grade, *we do*. But we need to understand writing as a process before we can deal with paper glut.

Writing is actually a *set of processes* for each writer. This is how Donna does it. Before she picks up a pen or sits down at the computer, she "begins" to write. Some call it prewriting, some call it planning. Donna used to call it another *p* word—*procrastination*. Donna's best writing involves some initial distancing. From the time she knows that she wants to—or has to—write something, she begins thinking about it. While driving along or loading the dishwasher, she thinks about it. While antiquing or wallpapering or planting flowers, she thinks about it. She may read about the subject or talk to colleagues about it. She keeps a tablet close by where she jots down ideas and "killer" words and phrases (which may or may not end up in the piece). If she is close to the computer when particularly salient thoughts arrive, she starts a list of these brain bursts. Sometimes she just sits at the computer and "lets it fly" as fast as her fingers can type. (When we first started working on this book, we stood in Donna's pool with water up to our shoulders, writing ideas and possible organizational schemes on tablets that quickly became soggy as our children cannon-balled into the deep end. It was a very hot summer.)

When Donna is ready to compose something, she thinks of the audience and purpose and writes her thoughts as she would speak them to that audience for that purpose. Her fingers move over the keyboard as she holds down her half of the conversation. She doesn't worry if it's in order, if it's spelled correctly, or if it hangs together. She just sets down a draft. Later she can take back anything she really doesn't mean, or want, to say. She can "Monday-morning-quarterback-it." She finds a great deal of liberation in knowing that she doesn't have to know what she wants to say before she says it.

After the piece, the section, the paragraph, or whatever unit she's working on is "said," Donna goes back and rereads it (often aloud) to see how it's working. Her revision strategies are recursive. Write a little—read a little—revise a little—edit a little. Before she quits a writing session, she jots down a few words about where she's going next with the piece. She often discovers what she has to say by writing it, rereading it, rewriting it, and thinking about it.

Before the piece is final, she prints out a hard copy. Invariably, it reads differently on a piece of paper than on the computer screen. Spell-check and grammar-check have tipped her off to editorial problems along the way, but she always finds things that her computer "missed" that bother her. So it's back to the keyboard to fine-tune.

At this point she unveils the piece of writing to a trusted "other"—someone who knows the audience and purpose and can give her feedback on how she is being "heard." Usually this person's feedback sends Donna back to the computer to make a few more changes—sometimes more than a few—before she prints out the final copy and sends it to the intended receiver.

Maybe you've recognized the above as being similar to stages of the writing process you've heard about elsewhere (Calkins 1986; Graves 1983, 1991; Hillocks 1987):

Prewriting—planning, listing, jotting, webbing, organizing, reading, outlining, making notes, figuring out what you might want to say.

Drafting—getting those preliminary thoughts onto paper in something that resembles connected text.

Revising—rereading and changing the piece to make the meaning clearer, to make sure it says what you want it to say.

Editing—rereading and making sure that mechanical features (i.e., punctuation, capitalization, spelling, grammar) are in order.

Publishing—sharing the piece with the intended audience.

You may also have heard this called *writing–rewriting–editing* or *planning–writing–publishing* or *fluency–form–correctness*. By whatever name, writing involves some kind of process. What kinds of processes and how many depend on the kind of writing a writer is doing.

Different Ways for Different Purposes

This leads us to a third understanding: different ways of and different purposes for writing. In real life the reasons we write fall into three major categories. Borrowing terminology used by Britton et al. (1975), Applebee (1984), and Lytle and Botel (1988), *personal* (or expressive), *informational* (or transactional), and *poetic* (or imaginative) writing fulfill different functions in our lives. Each of the three has its own audience and purpose in mind. A writer chooses among them according to particular purposes and audiences.

Personal (expressive) writing is "thinking on paper" for an audience of oneself. This is the stuff of journal writing, note taking, list making. Simply, you are writing for yourself—a comfortable audience who will not criticize you more than you can take. This is where you learn to feel comfortable with a pen or a keyboard, where you find your voice, where you discover that, yes, you can write. *Informational* (transactional) writing is "acting on the world," with an audience, necessarily, of others. It's the stuff of persuasion, information, explanation—the letters, essays, reports of traditional school writing. *Poetic* (imaginative) writing is creating art—poems, stories, plays, for example— also for an audience of others.

Historically schools have engaged students primarily in informational (transactional) writing, obscuring personal (expressive) writing, and sending poetic (imaginative) writing packing to English class. This is unfortunate. By giving short shrift to personal (expressive) writing, we ignore the very kind of writing that helps students find their voice and start to believe in themselves as writers. If they are not comfortable with personal writing, transactional and poetic writing may never become highly developed. Speaking of voice—why do students plagiarize? Is it because they are lazy, don't care, or like to cheat? Or is it because they never have found their own voices and the writings of others seem so much more compelling? We do a great disservice to our students when we don't engage them in personal writing.

The Moment You've Been Waiting For: Avoiding the Paper Glut

Our basic understanding about writing comprises four points:

- Students want to write.
- We have to give them frequent and regular opportunities to write.
- We have to engage them in the processes of writing.
- We have to give them opportunities to write for different purposes and audiences.

Teachers also need to sleep, eat, and keep from being buried under an avalanche of papers. Resolving these two seemingly opposite agendas seems impossible. But it's not.

First of all, not all writing needs to go through the whole process. Not everything is publishable. Slip in personal (expressive) writing as often as possible—prewriting or drafting, thinking aloud on paper. Don't grade it: it's not for you. It's for the audience of self. Second, invite poetic (imaginative) writing into your content area classes as an alternative way to respond to text. It will feel awkward at first: this has long been the private stock of English classes. (Trust us, the English teachers won't mind sharing.) However, having to make decisions about this kind of writing helps students zero in on what is most important about the content you're covering. In other words, use personal (expressive) and poetic (imaginative) writing as *ways of learning* in your class—*as means, not ends*. Third, reserve your grading for pieces written in the informational (transactional) mode. These are the pieces intended for an audience of others. By nature, they need to go through the whole process, becoming as clear and complete as possible. Even within this type of writing, you'll find that you can guide students into becoming better revisers and editors (both for themselves and for their peers), so that the pain of grading is lessened.

Thinking on Paper in Science: A Journey Begins

After two years of hearing Donna talk about writing being natural, a process, and requiring different forms, Roberta was still wary. She just couldn't get away from equating writing with 130 boring essays to read. *More* writing? She couldn't bear to think of adding still more things to grade to a pile of paperwork that already looked like the Leaning Tower of Pisa.

Roberta's past associations with writing had left her mired in the informational (transactional) mode; she had her students "act on the world" for an audience of "others," in this case, act on the teacher for a grade. It took some doing, but finally, with the help of some reading and a lot of examples, Roberta came to own the statement that "composing is a powerful learning process, writing helps students relate the new to the known—to connect their experiences and prior knowledge with the subject they are studying" (Lytle and Botel 1988, 50). In other words, personal (expressive) writing finally started to make sense! With renewed dedication she started the new school year resolved to integrate thinking on paper into her classroom.

No Deadwood Allowed

Roberta was intrigued by the journals and learning logs (Fulwiler 1987; Kirby 1981; Harste and Short 1988) that Donna was always talking about but was put off by their length. She had seen some journal writing done by students in elementary school and in middle school language arts classes: they went on for pages! Still, the basic idea seemed sound enough to try. She decided to do this type of writing in her classroom but to change the name. In her science class, these writings would be called *jottings*.

Now Roberta tells her students that learning *logs* sound like deadwood and she wants none of that in her room! *Jottings* connote something short and snappy: *Writing that isn't a finished-product. Doesn't need to go through all the stages of the writing process. Flashes of insight. Questions. Observations. Responses and reactions. A maximum of five minutes. Thinking on paper. For an audience of you.*

Jottings take many forms, so students tend not to become bored with them. They keep lined paper in their notebooks in a section called (need we say it) "Jottings." It's simple in the course of a lesson to ask them to turn to their jottings pages and write. They number their entries, so absentees easily figure out what they missed the day before. When do they write? Before, during, and after a reading, a lecture, a video, or a lab. What do they write? They predict what they think will happen, predict test questions, explain lab procedures in their own words, give examples of a video topic, produce Venn diagrams, create graphic organizers, problem-solve, voice opinions—the list goes on.

A jottings success story: Shelly was a very shy young lady who sat in the second seat in the second row. You've taught students like this. She never volunteered to participate and when called on she didn't answer loudly enough for anyone to hear. Although Roberta tries to get to know all 130 of her students, by November she still couldn't recognize Shelly's voice. One day Roberta asked the class to list everyday examples of filters in their jottings. During class discussion, Shelly volunteered several answers. Two days later, when Roberta asked students to give their opinions on a scientific issue, Shelly raised her hand and *read from her jottings.* This very shy girl became a confident participant when she could read her thoughts rather than answer spontaneously. Shelly began to share more and more when she had time to think on paper first, to find out what she had to say, to build confidence through rehearsal. Writing is built-in wait time, shown to be highly correlated with student thinking and response (Rowe 1974).

Monitoring Understanding

Roberta often has her students jot things down in order to monitor their own understanding. At the end of class, they often write about what they learned that period. At the beginning of the year, their work isn't impressive. A typical entry might read, "I learned about electrons and atoms today." In time, however, they become accustomed to demonstrating their knowledge to themselves, and the entries become more sophisticated, like this: "I learned about frequency and pitch today. Frequency is the number of vibrations per second and pitch is the highness or lowness of sound. They are related. Frequency determines pitch. The faster the frequency, the higher the pitch." As every real teacher knows, the end of a class period can be an invitation to all sorts of things. If the lesson ends early, potential troublemakers know just what to do with the extra time. If the office suddenly needs attendance information, homework for an absentee, and three weeks of assignments for the lucky student who will be traveling to Florida with his parents, they will need it *before the period ends.* Jottings to the rescue! Both students and their teacher make productive use of time.

Jottings also work well as an *after*-reading activity. Roberta's class had just read and discussed a magazine article on the scientific naming of animals. She asked them to pick out the five most important words or phrases in the article. After she listed them on the board, they reviewed their meanings. Next, she had them turn to their jottings pages and write a paragraph summarizing the article, using all five key words and phrases within that paragraph. When they had finished, students underlined the key words (and checked that they all were there), then shared with a partner what they had written. Finally, the whole class reviewed the meanings and discussed what they had written so that everyone could add to or delete from their work. This writing went through prewriting (identifying key words together), drafting (free-writing the paragraph), and revision (correcting information based on feedback from others), but no further. It served its purpose as thinking on paper, to help students monitor their comprehension.

Monitoring the Teacher!

One jottings experience was a real eye-opener for Roberta. Before a review for a test, she asked students to write what they *didn't* understand about the unit. So used to writing what they *knew*, they just stared ar her blankly. It was almost comical, a contest to see who would blink first! After more explanation and encouragement and several more minutes of perplexed looks, heads finally turned downward and pencils started to move. Circulating, Roberta read over their shoulders and used their comments to drive the ensuing review. Surprisingly, the same theme appeared in all three of her seventh-grade classes: they didn't understand the differences between parasites and saprophytes. Needless to say, Roberta rethought how to teach that topic the next time around.

Our colleague John uses a daily response sheet (see Figure 9–1) in his high school history classes. In addition to reiterating and summarizing, students are asked to go beyond the text to think about what they didn't understand, what they need to know more about, and what they see in a different light. John tells us this is by far the most valuable part of the response sheet and one that keeps him on his toes as a teacher. His students' curiosities stimulate his own research, and their observations shed interesting light.

Quotable Quotes and Honest Opinions

Like you, Roberta tries to tie current events to her subject area. Before she discovered the power of thinking on paper, she used to share a current event, then encourage class discussion. Some of her students discussed freely; many did not. Unhappy with the minimal involvement, she decided to move away from talk as the first response. She began to experiment with catchy quotations from the newspaper and other periodicals, placing them on the overhead—and later on the big-screen computer—and inviting students' response *in writing* first.

A favorite quotation is by scientist Melvin Cohn, who said, "I am grateful to be in a profession where the realization of being wrong is equivalent to an increase in learning" (1994). (We think this is also true about the teaching profession.) Through this one quote, Roberta was able to gather students' opinions and begin a discussion about the backbone of the field of science, the scientific method. Or again: in 1999, Surgeon General David Satcher said, "Because infectious diseases do not recognize borders, it is

A P HISTORY

DAILY RESPONSE SHEET

1. Pages read: _____ to _____

2. List three important facts or concepts found in today's reading:

THEY DO AT HOME AFTER THEY'VE READ THE ASSIGNMENT.

3. Write a paragraph of 4 or 5 sentences summarizing the most significant aspects of today's lesson.

THEY DO THESE DURING THE LAST 5–7 MINUTES OF CLASS. JOHN FINDS #4 TO BE THE MOST VALUABLE.

4. Write a sentence or two describing something you don't understand, something you would like more information about, or something you now see in a different light.

Figure 9–1. *John's daily response sheet*

increasingly necessary to protect the health and safety of American citizens by invest-ing in a global public health strategy." Little did he know that his statement would be-come a springboard for Roberta's science classes to debate the scientific and political implications of a global health strategy—*after* she had asked them to reflect on this issue in their personal writing.

Our world is ripe with news and opinions that relate to everything we do in school. We are a mirror of society at large. Social studies? Science? Health? Mathematics? Physical education and wellness? Technology? Ecology? Consumer Issues? Look no further than your daily newspaper. You'll recognize statements that support or refute key ideas and concepts in your content area. Bring them in, write about them, and debate them. It puts today's students in touch with past and present scientists, historians, politicians, mathematicians, athletes, and other giants who have affected and continue to affect knowledge in our fields.

　　Honest opinions are not limited to quotable quotes. Upcoming dissection labs give Roberta an opportunity to elicit students' opinions and beliefs through the safe forum of personal writing. By school policy, she must give students the choice of opting out of dissection labs if they or their family find them offensive. Before these labs begin, Roberta announces the topic Why Schools Have Students Do Dissection, and asks her students to reflect on possible reasons. She often chuckles at some of things they imagine: a chance for the teacher to take it easy and make kids do all the work? an opportunity to gross out the class? Thoughts like these occur frequently, along with some deeply felt opinions and beliefs. Students tell her things in writing that they might not feel comfortable saying face-to-face, and she respects that. After Roberta's students have expressed their opinions in writing that is graded only for effort and seen only by her, she presents her reasons for including dissection in her curriculum. Andrew expressed great resistance to dissection. After reading what he had written, Roberta spoke to his parents and to him, reassuring them that he would not be required to attend the labs. After Roberta had presented her explanation about why she has students dissect, Andrew's parents called to say he had changed his mind. He had told his parents, "Mrs. McManus has good reasons, and I think I'll do it." What could have become an uncomfortable situation for everyone was defused by the mutual respect that writing afforded.

Waxing Poetic

Yes, poetry in the content area. What'll we think of next? And we're not alone. Our colleague Brendan decided that social studies and poetry were a good match. To his students' amazement that he knew about such things, he explained the cinquain format:

(line one)	one noun (or noun phrase)
(line two)	two adjectives describing that noun
(line three)	three words describing action
(line four)	four words expressing feelings
(line five)	one noun that is a synonym for the noun in the first line

There was a catch, however. They couldn't write about just any subject. Their cinquain had to begin with one of the terms they were using in their unit on western expansion to the Mississippi: *steel plow, reaper, National Road, Erie Canal, steamboat,* and *steam locomotive.* Choose one of these and try it! We did, thus:

Reaper

Large, sharp

Moves, slashes, throws

Scary, threatening, ominous, replacement

Machine

To create this cinquain, we really had to "get inside" the time period and imagine how people might have felt about this invention—about its mechanism, about its girth, about its replacing manual labor.

Another of our favorite forms is the diamante. So often we deal with terms, ideas, or concepts in the content areas that are opposite in meaning. Sorting through these and making sure that students understand the attributes associated with each can be taxing. The diamante is an enjoyable playground on which to hone these attributes. The first half of the poem deals with one concept, while the second half deals with its opposite. The switch in concepts occurs in the middle of the fourth line. Here is the formula for this diamond-shaped poem:

one word (a noun, subject)

two words (adjectives describing line 1)

three words (*ing* or *ed* verbs relating to line 1)

four words (first two nouns relate to line 1; next two nouns relate to line 7)

three words (*ing* or *ed* words that relate to line 7)

two words (adjectives describing line 7)

one word (a noun, opposite of line 1)

Although the result is pleasant to the ear and eye, a significant review of the key ideas also takes place. The poet must understand the subjects well enough to describe them, tell how they move, and give key examples. Not bad, considering that students just think they're having fun! The closet poets in us just have to share our diamante with you!

Condensation

Unpleasant, soggy

Dropped, pelted, soaked

Rain, snow, sunshine, heat

Dried, aired, disappeared

Pleasant, welcomed

Evaporation

Haikus (five syllables, seven syllables, five syllables), limericks, and concrete poetry (written in such a way to outline the shape of the subject) are three more poetry forms that can find their way out of English class and into your content area. Your favorite English teacher probably would be delighted to share more with you and might even work with your students in a cooperative arrangement across disciplines.

Because of the economy of words in a poem, the writer must carefully consider every word choice. When we use poetry forms with students, we most often have them work in pairs. They discuss, sometimes argue, and revise until they have captured the essence of the subject in the most concise way. Meanwhile, a lot of synthesis of learning has taken place!

Listen, Stop, and Write

In the past Roberta's lessons followed this pattern:

ROBERTA: Lecture.

STUDENTS: Take notes.

ROBERTA: Give essay on test.

STUDENTS: Write incompletely and painfully.

ROBERTA: Get frustrated with the results.

Does this sound familiar? It was obvious to Roberta that something was lacking in the students' retention of the material and in their writing. So she experimented with a new kind of lesson plan. We call it *listen, stop, and write*. First Roberta told her students to open to their jottings pages but to put their pencils down. No note taking yet. Then she read to them for three minutes about the development of the first successful vaccination, by Edward Jenner, in 1796. (Every class has a student whose watch alarm goes off at the most inappropriate times; this young man became the timekeeper.) When the timekeeper yelled "Stop!" Roberta stopped midsentence and told everyone to write about what she had just read for the next two minutes while she watched the time. They started out hesitantly, but then their pencils began to fly across the page. When she called "Stop!" they put their pencils down, and the cycle started over again. They went through three cycles of *listen, stop and write*, then shared what they had written. In the process of sharing, they revised their notes, making additions and deletions so that their understanding was more complete. Afterward, they discussed this new process.

ROBERTA: What did you think of this new way of taking notes?

STUDENTS: It was easy.

JUSTIN: No, it's not. It's hard.

ROBERTA: Didn't it get easier the second and third time you did it?

STUDENTS: Much easier.

JUSTIN: No it didn't. It was hard the whole time.

ROBERTA: Did you watch TV last night, Justin?

JUSTIN: Yes.

ROBERTA: What did you watch? [Justin names a half-hour family comedy.] I missed that last night. Why don't you tell me about it? [Justin gives a detailed account of all that happened to the various characters in the show.] Class, is Justin correct? Did he do a good job summarizing the important points? [They all assure Justin that he has done a great job.] You know, Justin, even though I didn't see the episode, I feel that I now know everything that happened. You did a fabulous job of retelling the story of something that was on for thirty minutes over fourteen hours ago. I asked you to write about nine minutes of story you'd just heard. You *can* do this, and do it well!

Unfortunately, Justin continued to insist that her lesson was a tough one, but the rest of the students got the point that retelling a nine-minute story in their own words wasn't that hard to do. But Roberta wasn't finished. She was ready to give her students an assignment that needed to go through the complete writing process and be handed in for a grade. Intrigued? Read Chapter 10!

PURPOSEFUL WRITING TO AN AUDIENCE

Roberta was hooked on personal/expressive writing. Thinking on paper was so natural, and she used it in many ways, but the thought of asking her students to do informational/transactional writing still unnerved her. Writing like this needed to go through each step of the process. It would have to be *graded*.

Edward Jenner gave her the courage to try. Jenner, who developed the smallpox vaccine, is always of great interest to Roberta's seventh graders. Although he never visited the United States, a little village near their school bears his name—Jennersville—and is the site of the local hospital. Roberta told her class that she wanted to be sure that they had understood the previous listen-stop-and-write lesson on Jenner. She wanted them to write about Jenner's discovery, taking their essay through the entire writing process. They were not thrilled. She also told them that she absolutely was *not* in the mood to read boring essays; instead, she wanted to see some creativity. They were to write using a RAFT.

Floating on RAFTs

RAFT stands for *role, audience, format*, and *topic* (Santa 1988). In school students typically write in the *role* of students, for the *audience* of teacher, in the *format* of such things as the five-paragraph essay, on the *topic* of the teacher's choice. When students write only in the role of student for the audience of teacher, they often don't write very convincingly. They operate from a subconscious underlying assumption: *You're the teacher and you already know this stuff. So, if I sort of, kind of, string a few semiconvincing facts together, you'll fill in the blanks and make it make sense.* The motivation to write gets squelched further by the certainty that whatever they write, we will return it "dripping in blood." RAFT writing breaks these barriers down. In a RAFT assignment, students choose the role in which they want to write and the audience for whom they want to write. The format of the piece logically follows these decisions. Because the notions of audience and purpose are embedded within a RAFT assignment, students tend to write more thoroughly and convincingly.

When Roberta first introduced this idea, her class was puzzled. She became very nervous. After all, she was new at incorporating writing in science, and she was afraid the lesson would bomb. Taking a risk is never easy, especially in front of thirty squirrelly, judgmental teenagers. To reassure herself, she had gone over the lesson plan with reading specialist Lenetta ahead of time. Since Lenetta was so supportive, Roberta invited her to that first class in which she tried RAFT. (If you're going to fall on your face, do so in front of company so you won't suffer alone!)

To explain RAFTs, Roberta placed a set of choices (see Figure 10–1) on the board. Students could choose the *role*, *audience*, and *format* for their writing. Only the topic was nonnegotiable: they had to write about the first successful vaccination, in 1796, and it had to be at least one-and-a-half pages long. The class discussed the choices available, noting that some of the roles were historical persons, while others required them to use their imaginations and creativity. After much discussion, they got to work.

Roberta and Lenetta circulated, giving encouragement and answering questions. Heads were down and students were writing enthusiastically as fast as they could. Roberta and Lenetta smiled broadly—until they came to David. Unlike his peers, many of whom had three quarters of a page written already, David's page was blank. When they asked why he wasn't working, he said, "I'm thinking." Roberta suggested that he consult his jottings and get to work. After another circuit of the room, she approached David again. His paper was still pristine. As she started to admonish him for a lack of effort, Mary whipped around in her seat and said, "Leave him alone. He's thinking. He's a poet." Backing away, Roberta did as Mary said. The poet needed time to prewrite—to think—before he wrote.

This class met in the middle of the day and didn't end until the third lunch bell. When the third bell rang, not one student stood to leave. Lenetta and Roberta couldn't believe their eyes. They announced that it was the third bell and that the students needed to go to their next class. *Still no one moved.* They kept on writing. Finally, the two teachers said it was *their* lunch period, and since they were starving, the class had to scoot down the hall! Slowly, students rose to leave, except for Eddie who continued to write—and write—and write. Despite repeated urgings, Eddie continued until he was finished and, with a flourish, signed his name. He handed his paper to Roberta and said, "Now, grade this!" Delighted with his effort, she sent him on his way. She and Lenetta couldn't talk fast enough expressing their amazement at the students' response to this writing activity. They were so excited they ran to the phone and called Donna to pass on the good news! The next day Roberta introduced RAFTs to her other classes.

```
                        RAFT
R = role
A = audience
F = format
T = topic

ROLE
Edward Jenner
James Phipps
Sarah Nelms
Mrs. Nosey
newspaper reporter

AUDIENCE
?

FORMAT
diary
letter
dialogue
newspaper article
editorial
?

TOPIC
first successful vaccination in 1796—
a several-month-long procedure
```

Figure 10–1. *RAFT choices*

Revising RAFTs

Of course, the students asked for their graded papers back the day after they turned them in. But Roberta told them they would have to be patient. What they didn't know was that she had not collected their *finished* copies, only their first drafts. Having had so much success with writing in science so far, she decided she was ready to tackle the rest of the writing process.

When reading their drafts, Roberta was very sparing with her red pen. She read for content, writing positive comments and encouragement and refraining from marking every error. She held on to these papers for several days, then returned them. The students were dismayed to find no grades. When she told them these papers were not finished, they assured her that this work was their best and couldn't possibly be improved. She was ready for them. Remember the computer paper that came in one continuous series of connected sheets? Roberta had a draft of her own writing that was handwritten on six connected sheets of that paper. As it unfolded and fluttered to the floor, her cross-outs, scribbles, jottings in the margins, and even extra snippets of paper taped to strategic spots on the manuscript were plain to see. She explained that before she began writing at the computer, she literally cut and pasted when she revised her writing.

The students were puzzled about how they could do this with their own writing. So the *teacher-as-writer* began to describe where and why she had crossed out certain things, where the snippets of paper were before she attached them to her draft, and how she knew what changes needed to be made. They were hooked! Roberta told them that she often put a draft aside for a couple of days before looking at it again with a fresh eye—just as they had unknowingly done with the RAFT piece on Jenner. She encouraged them to read their pieces again with new eyes, and shared with them a revision strategy called ARMS, one based on strategies mature writers use when they revise (Faigley and Witte 1981):

A = Add something to the piece.

R = Remove something that isn't working anymore.

M = Move a portion of the text to another place where it will work better.

S = Substitute a word, a phrase, a sentence, an example to make it clear.

Wow! Teachers don't write everything correctly the first time? They have to revise, too? Gee, Mrs. McManus's draft looked really messy. She had to revise a lot. So how did you do that again? Such were the ahas that occurred within this community of writers sharing strategies. Through Roberta's example, students saw that writing is not finished until the writer is satisfied that the reader will understand it in the intended way.

As students were working at reseeing their writing, specific needs emerged. Roberta pulled eight students to the back of the room for a minilesson (Calkins 1994) because they had chosen newspaper articles as their format yet had included themselves in the writing. She talked with them about the more distant, objective stance that reporters take, and how they incorporate the five Ws—who, what, when, where, and why—at the opening of their articles. They looked at articles from *The Philadelphia Inquirer* to prove this point. Roberta also noticed that many students were using contemporary slang: "Hey, Dude, what's up?" and "See ya later." Quickly, she taught a minilesson about the type of discourse that might have been used in the late 1700's. Formal salutations and closings such as "My dearest mother" and "Your most obedient servant" quickly became commonplace. One young lady decided to keep the best of both worlds by having newscasters Connie Chung and Jane Pauley go back in time to interview the people of Jenner's village (see Figure 10–2). A budding science fiction writer at work!

After her minilessons, Roberta paired students who had exhibited the same need and had them work as revision partners, reading each other's drafts and advising each other on their modifications. (Since she first introduced the Jenner RAFT assignment, her school has begun grouping students by teams. Roberta and the language arts teacher for the team now work together to help students with revision and editing strategies for this assignment.)

Revision work for this assignment is never limited to stylistics, however. Roberta's superordinate goal for her students is that they know the science of Jenner's work. With this in mind, she developed a one-page revision checklist for students to use to make sure they have the correct scientific information (see Figure 10–3). Incorporating literacy into the content areas does *not* mean that the teacher must jettison content. Instead, literacy and content work together. Denise's letter from James Phipps' mother to his father captured both creativity and science content (see Figure 10–4).

Cleaning Up the RAFTs and Getting Them Ready to Sail

Students enjoyed sharing their pieces with each other in the revision stage. Interest was high, as they saw how someone else chose to present the same information. They were quick to double-check each other about scientific accuracy and offered good suggestions to make the emerging RAFTs even better. Then Roberta told them it was time to make sure that the mechanical parts of their writings were in as good shape as their wonderful content. In other words, it was time to edit.

Before the protests could rise, Roberta told everyone to read his or her piece aloud because it is easier to locate what needs to be fixed this way. (If you don't believe it, try it with your next piece of writing!) Sure enough, the hubbub of reading that followed was interrupted only by writers stopping to insert words, punctuation marks, and correct spellings. The ear really does correct what the eye misses! Following this, Roberta gave each person an editing checklist (see Figure 10–5). This checklist was a combination of things she had learned from the language arts teachers of these students and her own pet peeves—things that drove her crazy when she saw them in student writing. Notice that there are three response columns—the writer, a friend, and the teacher. Roberta encouraged the students to feel free to substitute a parent for "friend" to help them edit their final copy. She hoped that by the time the final products got to her, they would have been already edited by two people and would be in good shape.

Roberta was amazed by the creativity that bubbled up in her students. They caught the spirit of this activity and helped one another decide the most effective ways to present their final drafts. Some of the letter writers turned in letters in envelopes complete with address and hand-drawn stamps. Series of letters were common, and arrived on her desk

JANE PAULEY:	We are here at the workplace of Dr. Edward Jenner where he is going to try out a new theory. Let's go talk to Mr. Jenner about what's going to be going on. Mr. Jenner, what exactly is going on here today?
EDWARD JENNER:	Well Jane, we are going to test this eight-year-old boy by making incisions in his arm. We are going to use pus from a young milk-maid, Sarah Nelms, and apply the pus to the incisions.
JANE PAULEY:	What do you hope to accomplish by this?
EDWARD JENNER:	I hope to prove that by having cowpox you will be immune to smallpox.
[One hour later]	
JANE PAULEY:	Dr. Jenner is now making the incision into James' arm. The pus has now been applied. We now have to wait until the cowpox gets into his system.
[One week later]	
JANE PAULEY:	James has cowpox with a slight fever and a few blisters. We now go to Connie Chung for some information on Dr. Edward Jenner.
CONNIE CHUNG:	His schooling was at home until he attended a local grammar school. At the age of twelve, he was an apprentice for a surgeon. Then he went to St. George's Hospital to study more. It was not until he was forty-nine that he applied for his M.D. and was the first person to use the word *virus*.
JANE PAULEY:	Dr. Jenner is now making two more incisions into James' arm and is applying smallpox pus to his arm. It seems James is going through a bit of pain. We will be reporting on this when the results of the experiment are final.
[Two weeks later]	
JANE PAULEY:	It seems Dr. Jenner has done it. James has no signs of smallpox, therefore meaning that James is immune to smallpox. Let's go to Connie and talk with Dr. Jenner on how he feels about this amazing new discovery.
CONNIE CHUNG:	Dr. Jenner, how do you feel about this exciting and remarkable discovery?
DR. JENNER:	Well, I feel great! I feel I have saved the world from the deadly disease and have made my mom real proud.
CONNIE CHUNG:	Well, there you have it, straight from Dr. Edward Jenner. Back to you, Jane.
JANE PAULEY:	Well, standing next to me is a very brave young man, James Phipps. James, how do you feel about what you have done?
JAMES PHIPPS:	Well, it hurt, but I guess I helped everybody out by doing it.
JANE PAULEY:	Well, that's all we have time for today. Tune in tomorrow for a special interview with George Washington. Thank you for watching CBS News.

Figure 10–2. *Amy's RAFT work*

Science 7   Physician _____

CHECK IT OUT!

We've been talking, listening, and writing about Edward Jenner and his work. It's now time for you to check out your understanding and knowledge! Write "yes" or "no" in the answer blanks.

_____ 1. Is smallpox a serious disease?

_____ 2. Is cowpox a serious disease?

_____ 3. Did James Phipps get cowpox?

_____ 4. Did James Phipps get smallpox?

_____ 5. Was everyone living in Jenner's time likely to get smallpox?

_____ 6. Was everyone living in Jenner's time likely to die of smallpox?

_____ 7. Was Jenner a doctor with a medical degree?

_____ 8. Did Jenner visit America?

_____ 9. Did Jenner inoculate James Phipps with both cowpox and smallpox?

_____ 10. Did Jenner give James Phipps any shots?

_____ 11. Did Jenner's first successful vaccination take place over several months?

_____ 12. Did Jenner's discovery result after years of laboratory research?

_____ 13. Did Jenner prove that cowpox gave immunity to smallpox?

_____ 14. Was Jenner the first person to notice that milkmaids never caught small-pox?

_____ 15. Was Jenner the first to act on the countryside belief that milkmaids never got smallpox?

_____ 16. Did Sarah Nelms get smallpox?

_____ 17. Has smallpox been wiped off the earth?

_____ 18. Does PA law still require students to get smallpox vaccinations?

Figure 10–3. *Checklist for Jenner information*

Dear Charles,

You will never guess what happened in the past two months. I decided to wait until it was all over to tell you. Now, you have to promise that you won't get mad when I tell you. Do you promise? Okay, here's the situation.

Edward and Elaine Jenner (Ed's new wife) came over. Ed was so excited! He was telling me that he might have discovered a vaccination for smallpox! Isn't that great? I was always worried that little Jimmy would get that. You know how deadly that is. Well anyway, Ed told me he needed a volunteer to demonstrate his experiment. So, naturally, I volunteered little Jimmy! Now, calm down, sweetie! I know what you're thinking. I trusted Ed. He was careful with Jimmy. He treated him like his own son. So anyway, Jimmy is just fine! He's still the same little boy! He misses you. I do, too. If only you didn't have to go into the Army. They shouldn't have taken you. But, in two more years, you'll be out!

I will explain the procedure to you briefly. On January 21, 1796, I took Jimmy to Ed's office in town. There was a woman there by the name of Sarah Nelms. She was a milkmaid at the Johnson farm and she got cowpox from the cows. Ed realized that milkmaids who got cowpox never got smallpox. So, after some studying, he realized that it just might be true. So, he tied Jimmy down in a chair, and put two slits in his arm. Then he rubbed the cowpox in (pus from Sarah's blisters). Jimmy got a fever. Several weeks later, Ed rubbed the smallpox in new slits. (I held my breath!) We waited and waited and nothing happened. On March 12, 1796, Ed and a few other doctors and scientists came to town, and carefully looked over Jimmy. And, now it is official that Edward Jenner has discovered the first vaccination for smallpox! And Jimmy couldn't be healthier! In fact, he will never get smallpox! He has something called an active acquired immunity. I'm sorry for not consulting you first. I love you!

P.S. I can't wait to see you on Spring Break! Until then, please write me back!

Love always,
Mary Phipps

Figure 10–4. *Denise's RAFT letter*

EDITING CHECKLIST

	myself	friend	teacher

English Usage

1. A capital letter begins each sentence.   _____ _____ _____
2. Each sentence ends with a punctuation mark.   _____ _____ _____
3. Each sentence is complete—it has a subject
   and a verb.   _____ _____ _____
4. No run-on sentences.   _____ _____ _____
5. Keep the verb tense the same in all sentences—
   easiest to write in past tense.   _____ _____ _____
6. Spelling is correct.   _____ _____ _____

Paragraphs

1. Indentation at beginning.   _____ _____ _____
2. First sentence should be the main idea.   _____ _____ _____
3. All other sentences should support, describe,
   or explain the main idea by listing, example,
   identification.   _____ _____ _____
4. Every new main idea should be a new paragraph.   _____ _____ _____
5. Paragraphs DO NOT have to be long.   _____ _____ _____

Science content

1. Each sentence makes sense.   _____ _____ _____
2. Each sentence keeps to the topic.   _____ _____ _____
3. Each idea is accurate.   _____ _____ _____
4. Details are presented in the proper sequence.   _____ _____ _____
5. All important information is included.   _____ _____ _____

Neatness

1. Handwriting is neat.   _____ _____ _____
2. Red ink is not used.   _____ _____ _____
3. Margins are straight.   _____ _____ _____
4. Papers are not "doodled" on.   _____ _____ _____

Figure 10–5. *Individual editing checklist*

tied with ribbons. Those using a diary format presented their work in cloth-covered cardboard bound together with stitches. One enterprising young lady sewed a pocket to the inside jacket of the diary. In it was a medical release form signed by a make-believe Mary Phipps, the mother of the child on whom Jenner had experimented—a certain reflection of what that student knows about our litigious society today! Newspaper articles appeared with advertisements for products of the era. Many times, students tea-dyed paper or burnt it around the edges to simulate old paper. We still chuckle over one young man's story of trying to age his composition paper by burning. Twice he wrote his final copy, then tried to burn the edges; twice he caught his paper on fire and destroyed his final draft. He finally decided to burn the paper *first*, then write—a story Roberta remembers to tell her students now whenever they want to "age" paper for a writing assignment!

Did the RAFT Sink or Float? (Aka Grading)

Since this piece of writing went through the entire process, Roberta graded it. Instead of 130 boring essays, she received very interesting and well-done pieces. But she faced the age-old problem: how to grade them fairly, staying focused and maintaining the same standards from the first paper to the last. She talked to language arts teachers in her building and several elementary teachers, assuming that they had the answers. Taking their best advice and adding her concern for scientific accuracy, she had developed the editing checklist she gave to students (Figure 10–5), but she decided this was too cumbersome to use as a grading tool. She was spending too much time on the checklist when her teacher intuition had already had told her the overall grade the paper deserved. She realized it needed to be shortened. After several permutations, she settled on the system for evaluating the Jenner RAFTs shown in Figure 10–6. (Frankly, she was pretty pleased with herself. Later, at a conference, she found out there is a name for what she had developed through her teacher intuition—-*rubrics*. She was crushed, because she had been certain it was her idea!)

Some of the best writing Roberta had ever seen from middle schoolers grew out of this assignment. Why? The literature on writing has pointed again and again to *choice* and *ownership* as keys to powerful writing (Graves 1983; Atwell 1987; Calkins 1994). Roberta's experience here confirms this. Only the topic and length were mandated, and as it turned out, length was not an issue. They wanted to write more and more and more. Five pages were common. Not only that, the students' responses to an essay question about Jenner on the next exam were superb. They knew the topic, had manipulated and owned the information, and retained it.

A few years after Roberta began incorporating the Jenner RAFT assignment into her teaching, the local hospital decided to dedicate a plaque to Jenner and name a prestigious award after him. The ensuing press coverage prompted many of her former students, by then in high school and beyond, to contact her and send newspaper clippings to make sure she knew about it! Obviously, the information had "stuck."

Grading System for "RAFT" Assignment on Edward Jenner

SCIENCE CONTENT

Details are in proper sequence   /5
All important information is included   /5
Information is accurate   /5

GRAMMAR & SPELLING

Complete sentences; tenses   /3
Punctuation   /3
Spelling   /3
Good paragraphs   /3

NEATNESS   /3

CREATIVITY   /3

total   /33

GRADE   _____

comments:

Figure 10–6.   *Rubric for grading the RAFT on Jenner*

Extra! Extra! Read All About It!

Students seem to like writing in newspaper format, but as Roberta has found in the RAFT assignments, they don't necessarily have a strong frame of reference for journalism. Alexander Fleming, who discovered penicillin, was big news in his time and beyond.

He presented an opportunity to do more newspaper writing. First, however, Roberta used the listen-stop-and-write strategy (see Chapter 9) as she read aloud several articles about the discovery of the first antibiotic. After students had their notes in hand, she gave the assignment: they were to write a newspaper article about the discovery and use of penicillin. There were a number of choices to make. Would they set their article in 1928, when Fleming discovered a secretion from the mold *penicillium* and thought it was a curiosity? Or would they tell about it from the perspective of 1945, when Fleming, Howard Florey, and Ernst Chain won the Nobel Prize in Medicine for the development and production of penicillin? Or would they choose to write an obituary on the 1955 date of Fleming's death? The catch was the information had to be presented true to the year in which it supposedly was written.

After looking at sections of the *Philadelphia Inquirer* to investigate journalistic style for both articles and obituaries, the students set to work. Their work was amazing. Many students were not satisfied with the information from their listen-stop-and-write jottings and did more research on their own. Those with computer access set their articles in columns with justified margins; those without computers handwrote their pieces using carefully aligned columns as well. Several students pasted in a newspaper photo of someone whom they thought "looked scientific." In one case, that was a picture of a local school board member who had just been featured in the local paper. (We made sure he received a copy of this student's work. Interestingly, this gentleman *was* a scientist—but a geologist, not a pathologist.) We all enjoyed this one!

Time-Travel Letters

We're sure most grandparents would agree that their grandchildren don't send them enough letters. Some have even lamented that letter writing is a lost art. Roberta was surprised to find that many of her students didn't know the basic parts of a letter, let alone how to construct one. Wait—let's qualify that. They don't *transfer* their letter-writing knowledge from language arts class to science, except for passing notes across three rows of seats asking who will go with whom to the next dance.

Letter writing requires students to think of both audience and purpose, two key elements in strong writing. Often, students provide more detail in a chatty letter than they do in an essay or report. Finding inspiration in the book *Cranial Creations* (Downing and Miller 1990), Roberta taught the structure of a letter by examining one that supposedly traveled from 1721 through time from Anton van Leeuwenhoek.

With a copy of the letter on the overhead projector and in each student's hands, Roberta labeled its return address, salutation, body, and closing. The students' task was to write a return letter. They numbered the questions that van Leeuwenhoek wanted to have answered, examined the rubric by which their work would be assessed, and began to formulate their responses. They took this assignment to language arts class with them, where Roberta's colleague worked with them on the revision and editing stages. Four days later they proudly handed in their final products to Roberta. Many had gone beyond the initial assignment, turning in their letters in addressed envelopes and including drawings of their own to help explain the advances in science.

The possibilities for time-travel letters are endless. Did you know that Thomas Edison invented the ditto machine? Couldn't he write a letter asking for an update on copying methods? Wouldn't Alexander Graham Bell be astounded by the Internet? What would our founding fathers think of the interpretation of the Constitution by today's Supreme Court? Could Newton have foreseen the current applications of his new mathematics called calculus? Letters between one or more of the presidents carved into Mount Rushmore and the current resident of 1600 Pennsylvania Avenue, Washington, D.C., comparing presidencies could be quite interesting. Stephen King and William Shakespeare might surprise us with their conversations about popular fiction of their times. And just imagine a series of letters between Mozart and a contemporary rapper comparing their interpretations and inspirations for music. Try it! Letter writing demands clarity. A letter is going to someone—even if it's a pretend someone—for some reason; it has to be clear.

From English Class to Science Class

In addition to assigning complete pieces of writing, Roberta tries to teach opportunistically about language. Whenever possible, she brings talk about such things as sentences and paragraphs into her science classes. (We know that English/language arts teachers teach sentences and paragraphs, in spite of students' protests that they have no idea what they are. For some reason, students leave behind their understanding of these things when they walk out the English/language arts classroom door. It's the issue of transfer once again.) Here are some of the ways we've found to shore up their learning across the curriculum, to help that understanding slip out of the English classroom door and into the content areas.

Let's Talk Sentences

Early on, Roberta figured out that one easy way to integrate writing across the curriculum was to stop asking so many questions that require one-word answers. She used to ask questions like this:

> [Accompanying a picture of three beakers] These three beakers all contain water. A different powder has been added to each one. Which beaker contains the solution?

By using eeny-meeny-miney-moe, students had a one-in-three chance of answering that question correctly without even thinking about the science involved. Her revised version of this question now asks students to *give two reasons* for their answer and to respond *in complete sentences*. After a good bit of frustration at asking for complete sentences and not getting them, one day she turned to the board and began diagramming a sentence. When she wrote *subject* and *verb*, one astonished young man hollered out, "Gee Mrs. McManus—you know about those too?" Didn't they realize she was a literate adult? Slapping her forehead for her own assumptive teaching, she realized that she would have to make her point more clearly and regularly. Thus began her standard phrasing, "Use a complete sentence—you know, a subject and a verb." After repeating this for the umpteenth time, she knew that she had gotten through to one class. She started with "Use a complete sentence—" and they, in sing-song little voices, chanted, "—we know, a subject and a verb"!

Paragraph Progress

Social studies teacher Brendan's review circles (see Figure 10–7), on the surface, look like a content review. He gives students the word clues and they have to identify what he's talking about. That in itself would serve his social studies purposes well, but he doesn't stop there. Seeing an opportunity to reinforce paragraph unity, he has students take these clues and develop them into a coherent paragraph, using the names of the men as the topic and the clues as details for the supporting sentences. After a bit of practice, he reverses the procedure and gives them the topic. They have to come up with the clues (aka details for the supporting sentences), then develop a paragraph on each. Notice that he requires at least one verb to prime their sentences to show action. Verbs? Paragraphs? Social studies? After the typical surprise that he knows such things, students begin to transfer their language arts learning from one class to the next.

QAD Revisited

As promised in Chapter 6, we're going to revisit QAD (Question, Answer, Details). In addition to working well in guiding reading, it really helps students understand how to use paragraphs within longer pieces of text. Roberta used to ask students to write summaries and then bang her head against the wall. Instead of comprehensive and well-organized summaries, they would write about miniscule details that caught their eye, or they would tell all about the first thing they learned through the reading, lecture, or video, and nothing else. Worst of all, they were packaged in monstrously long single paragraphs.

Smoking brought an end to this. No, Roberta didn't take up the habit in frustration; she showed a video on smoking. After the video, she asked students to write a summary of what they had learned. The monster paragraphs rolled in, none of them capturing the essence of a summary. That night, she rethought QAD. What would happen if she used it to structure their note taking so that they would see the difference between main idea and details? What if she gave them the basic skeleton of a summary and had them add the pieces? Would this help? It was worth a try. The next day, she talked to her classes about why their summaries were not sufficient, and told them that they were going to write them again. (You can imagine the moans and eye rolls that greeted this news.) This time, she told them, she was going to help them understand what a summary in science should look like by giving them a QAD guide (see Figure 10–8).

What a difference! The Q, A, and D columns guided their note taking, helping them identify the important information and keeping them focused throughout the entire video. With those notes in hand, writing a cogent summary was easy. Each question signaled the beginning of a new paragraph. Within each paragraph, the A column represented the topic sentence while the D column contained the details. As a result, their second summary-writing experience was much more productive. Roberta then had them compare their two pieces of writing and discuss the differences. Clearly, her specific directions had helped them write their stellar summaries about smoking, but there was broader learning going on. By carefully structuring the paragraphing-and-summarizing activity, she had given students the opportunity to create their own models. The contrast between their two attempts at summarizing was a powerful learning experience!

Coming to Terms with Assessment

Grading is never easy, as any real teacher can tell you, but rubrics certainly make it easier. First of all, they force us to come to terms with how we define "quality writing" in any particular piece. Although we always have an amorphous idea of what that is—often stored in our minds as "I'll know it when I see it"—rubrics formalize this into criteria that both students and teacher can understand. Second, they let students know ahead of time what the expectations for this piece of writing are. Students not only write *this piece* better but also learn things about good writing that they can use in future pieces.

Roberta remembers the first time she returned writing with the rubric attached. Jamil pulled reading specialist Lenetta aside:

JAMIL: Is this what she used to grade my work?

LENETTA: Yes. Are you happy with your B?

JAMIL: You mean, she read my paper and graded these exact things?

LENETTA: Yes.

JAMIL: So this is exactly where I got points taken off?

LENETTA: Yes. Isn't this a good system?

JAMIL: You mean to tell me that she didn't just read it and give me a B?

In other words, Jamil was pleased to know exactly where he did well, where he fell down, and where he could improve next time.

When we evaluate, our feedback should do more than pronounce judgment. Of course, that's easy to say when it's the middle of summer and we're not looking at 130 papers to grade. We know how easily the urge to write *Nice job. Grade = A*, or *This is not your best work! Grade = D* can overtake us when we're in the midst of a busy school

DIRECTIONS: From the clues given, identify the men and write their names on the lines provided. Then, using the words in the circle, write two paragraphs identifying and explaining the importance of each.

Figure 10–7. *Brendan's review circles*

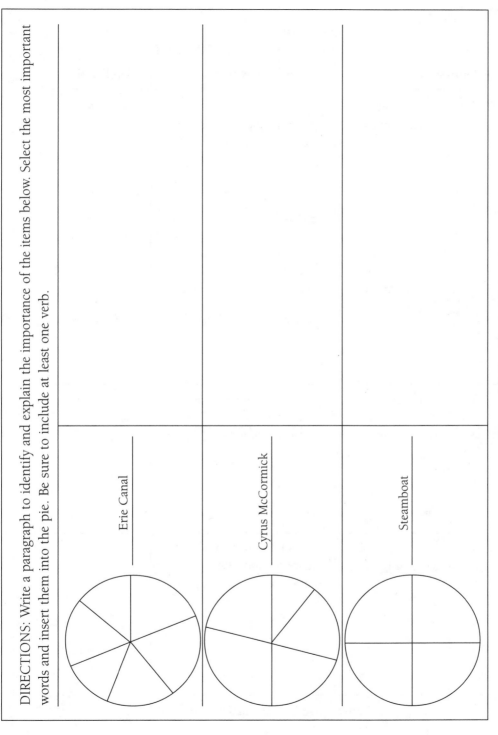

DIRECTIONS: Write a paragraph to identify and explain the importance of the items below. Select the most important words and insert them into the pie. Be sure to include at least one verb.

Erie Canal

Cyrus McCormick

Steamboat

Figure 10–7. *(Continued)*

QAD—MOVIE SUMMARY
"SMOKING, PAST & PRESENT"

Q (Question)	A (Answer)	D (Detail)
1. What is the topic of my first paragraph?	Tobacco was originally grown in the Americas and then introduced to Europe.	
2. What is the topic of my second paragraph?	As time went on attitudes toward smoking changed.	
3. What is the topic of my third paragraph?	Cigarette machines made more cigarettes available to more smokers.	
4. What is the topic of my fourth paragraph?	It has been proven that cigarette smoking is dangerous to your health.	

Figure 10–8. *QAD guide for summarizing*

year. We both have found, however, that rubrics help us not only determine a grade but also give students useful feedback. And in the broader picture, everything we do should move students toward growing competence in writing.

UGHS, AWKS, and AHAS

We heard Beverly Bimes-Michalak (1990) describe the UGHS, AWKS, and AHAS of responding to students' writing. UGHS refer to things we write on their papers like "Messy!" "You can do better!" "Terrible!" There also are "positive" UGHS, however, summary comments like "Good work!" or "Terrific!" All in all, these comments do not improve writing; they just proclaim our judgment calls. AWKS are only a little bit better. They're the classic things that have been written on scores of papers for years: "AWK," "run-on," and "frag." Useful feedback? Yes, in an editorial sense, but not in terms of improving the power of the writer's voice. What improves the content of writing, the voice of the author, and his ability to get his points across to the reader, are the AHAS. AHAS are comments we write from our hearts *as readers*, comments that let the writer know how he is being read. "I am laughing out loud" packs more punch than "Good use of humor." "I can picture this vividly in my mind's eye, and I'm feeling scared" is more informative than "Good description." "I'm confused here" tells the writer that she needs to rework a sentence much better than "AWK" or "run-on." "So what did she *do*??" lets the writer know that she needs a verb to accompany this "frag." Writing gets better when the *reader* in us responds.

They All Want to Write—Will We Let Them Get Good at It?

After writing had become a regular part of science class, Roberta called Donna one night and said, "I have to read you this quote. It says exactly what I've been thinking." The speaker was Bob Tierney, himself a science teacher who weaves writing into the fabric of his classes. Reflecting on using writing to learn, he said,

> I found I was hearing my students' real voice for the first time in my career. I used to hear the voice they used to get the grade; the voice that wrote, "Clams are very important to our society. . . ." Now I hear the voice that writes, "I hate clams. I don't like 'em, but the way they breathe is. . . ." (1984, 8)

Students have strong voices that they want to use—if we let them. Not only that, they use these voices to get the grades. Not just grades on their written assignments, but better grades on exams and in class participation. Writing actively engages everyone, not just the two or three who choose to raise their hands and stay involved in what goes on in the classroom. When students write, they have to think. When they think, they internalize information, using the vocabulary and concepts of science rather than just listening to Roberta use them. When they internalize information, they *know*.

Roberta truly regrets that she put off incorporating writing for so long. (Donna, of course, resists saying, "I told you so!") Making students feel comfortable with their own voice and helping them believe in themselves as writers is a lifelong gift we can give. And in the process, we give them permission to manipulate the content we so desperately want them to know.

CHAPTER 11

LEARNING FOR A LIFETIME

Real teachers are saddled with an enormous responsibility. We not only have to instill in our students a knowledge of our content area, we also have to prepare them for *real life*. Of course we hope our students will go out into the world to use many of the truths we have so deliberately taught them about history or science or whatever. But their real challenge will be to function as employees and employers, spouses and parents, neighbors and community members of worth. We must make sure that they are up to it.

It is so easy to become caught up in content. We know the clutch we feel when we look at the calendar and our curriculum and find that they do not match. There always is so much more that we need to teach! But if we can sidestep that for a moment, let's project ten or fifteen years into the future. Our then-grown-up students will need to be able to seek, organize, and draw connections within a body of knowledge that keeps growing exponentially. They will need to work with others to maneuver the synthesis and application of that knowledge in their real worlds. They will need to be able to communicate and interact effectively with those around them. We wish them the preparedness to do these things well. Above all, we wish them a healthy balance in their lives so that they *live life* rather than just *get through it*.

Our personal wish list for our students' futures, interestingly, is not very different from the preparedness that Fortune 500 companies say they want for their employees. A survey conducted by the American Society for Training and Development (ASTD) and the U.S. Department of Labor (2001) identifies these top-ten job skills:

1. Teamwork.
2. Problem solving.
3. Interpersonal skills.
4. Oral communication.

5. Listening.
6. Creative thinking.
7. Leadership.
8. Writing.
9. Computation.
10. Reading.

Although it may pain us, no one is calling for the isolated bits of regurgitated knowledge, individually acquired, that we so often mete out in real schools. The National Association of Colleges and Employers (NACE) asked 435 employers to respond to a survey, *Job Outlook 2000*, and found that *interpersonal skills* topped the list of skills they valued in a job candidate, with *teamwork skills* and *verbal communication skills* following closely. According to Marilyn Mackes, NACE's executive director, "It's not enough for a candidate to have knowledge—the candidate has to be able to share that knowledge effectively and tactfully in order for the company to succeed" (NACE 2000, 1).

Real life requires bigger things—processes and habits of mind. We often hear the call to include study-skills programs in the curriculum as a way to instill such things, yet we reject these isolated programs. While there are many well-intentioned minicourses in note taking, outlining, and test taking, our sense is that the skills promulgated in these isolated programs don't transfer to real life. *Not that we reject study skills.* On the contrary, the activities we propose in this book (and others like them) embed traditional study skills directly within the context of the content being taught *at the time it's being taught.* Getting through individual lessons, assignments, and courses is all well and good, but to help our students function well in real life, we need to seek opportunities within our curricula to engage them in the types of activities and projects they will encounter when they leave us.

Learning to Look It Up and Tell About It

Roberta really stretched her comfort zone by becoming a de facto teacher of reading, not to mention making the gigantic leap to becoming a teacher of writing. Having built her confidence, she decided to brave another new frontier: student research and student speeches. Not that she hadn't done these things before her conversion experience: she had, with varying levels of frustration, and had discontinued them. Armed with her new understanding about providing scaffolds to help her students do what she asked them to do, she began assigning research and speech projects once again.

She broached the subject of a research project about animals to her sixth-grade classes. The groans were nothing compared with the howls of protest when she explained that their research would culminate in a speech to the class. Guttural groans. Loud howls. Was she out of her mind? Wisely, she talked with them and listened to the causes of their distress.

She asked them one question: *Why are you upset about this?* She was peppered with their questions in response: *How long does the speech have to be? How much research do we have to do? How many sources do we have to have? How much information do you want? Where do we get the information? Does this count? How are you going to grade it? Can't we just write a report and not do the speech? No? Then can we write out our speech and just read it? What do you mean, we can only use one index card for our speech?* It wasn't that they weren't willing to do the work. They didn't know *how*, at least not in science class. Their concerns fit into two categories: how to know when their research was complete, and how to fold all of that research into a speech. Which seems a lifelike enough problem to us. Think ten years into the future. These same students are starting careers. Their job calls for them to investigate something and then tell the rest of the employees what they found out.

Roberta decided to model, step-by-step, how a mature adult goes about researching and presenting. For this assignment, she decided to construct a note-taking guide (see Figure 11–1) to ease their fears about researching information from print sources. Each box of the guide contained a type of information she wanted them to seek, with one box purposely reserved for interesting facts that caught their eye. They would know that they were done when all the boxes were filled. Taking this a step further, she had filled in her own research about the leopard frog. Armed with a bit more confidence, students set off for the library.

After successfully gathering information, they were still very uncertain about how to convert their completed boxes of notes into a speech. So the next day Roberta gave them a plan of attack (see Figure 11–2). Then using her research guide, she presented her speech about the leopard frog, careful to incorporate all the positive qualities of speechmakers. However, she also modeled a bad speech. Much to the delight of her students, she tripped blithely into the pitfalls that can topple speechmakers—hair twirling, overuse of *um* and *ah*, blanking out, speaking too quickly, total lack of eye contact, pacing about, and other nervous tics that drive an audience crazy. Being able to laugh at her comical routine always defuses some of the anxiety students are feeling and, at the same time, underscores the difference between good and bad speechmaking behavior.

Roberta always follows her presentations about appropriate speechmaking techniques by talking about proper audience behavior. After listing attributes of good audiences in Sam's class, she assured her charges that she would model *bad* audience behavior if a student required it. Leaving them guessing what she meant by that, she invited the first speaker to begin. Real teachers, you've all had a Sam in your class. He's the one who pushes the envelope by being extremely disruptive during a classmate's speech, in spite of your best teacher stares. When it was Sam's turn, he was totally surprised when Roberta sailed a paper airplane to the front of the room and crashed a row of books off the bookshelf, distracting him from the flow of his speech just as he had done to his

ANIMAL SPEECH - RESEARCH PAGE   Researcher <u>MRS. McMANUS</u>
"Leopard Frog"

Describe your animal. (What does it look like?)

ABOUT 6 INCHES LONG

TOP: GREEN + SPOTTED } TO HIDE
BOTTOM: WHITE   } FROM
                       } ENEMIES

Food - What does your animal eat?
      How does it eat?

— INSECTS
— FLIPS OUT STICKY TONGUE,
  CATCHES INSECTS + PULLS
  INTO MOUTH STABS WITH
  2 BIG TEETH + SWALLOWS

Where does your animal live?

NORTH AMERICA
(EXCEPT DESERTS)

Could it be found in Oxford?

YES

Describe the environment.

YOUNG — LIVES IN FRESH WATER,
    (POND, CREEK, RIVER, LAKE, etc.)
OLD — LIVES ON LAND

How does your animal move?

SWIMS + JUMPS WITH ITS POWERFUL BACK LEGS
BACK LEGS HAVE WEBS BETWEEN THE TOES
    TO HELP WITH SWIMMING

Is there anything special or different about your animal? List and explain the special things here.

FROGS ARE AMPHIBIANS - "DOUBLE LIVING"
    YOUNG IN WATER, OLD ON LAND
    YOUNG WITH GILLS, OLD WITH LUNGS
LIFE CYCLE = EGG → TADPOLE → FROG
HIBERNATE IN WINTER
COLD-BLOODED

Figure 11–1. *A guide to aid research*

Plan of Attack for Your Animal Speech

1. Do a good job on your animal research page. Try to use one encyclopedia and at least one book.

2. Next, use arrows or numbers on your research page to show the FLOW that you want your speech to have. (Connect your boxes.)

3. Now, write a report using your research page as a guide.

4. Read your report out loud several times. Be a friendly editor. Make additions and deletions. Should you shift any information to another location?

5. Pick out the most important parts of your report and make notes on an index card. (Ask for help if you need it.)

6. Now, practice your speech out loud several times using your index card as a guide. (You may look at this card in class but you may NOT read from it.)

7. Can you draw a picture of your animal to show your class during your speech?

Figure 11–2. *Plan of attack*

classmate! After the speech, Sam apologized to his classmates. Then he sat down, assumed a military posture with hands folded on the desk, winked at Roberta, and said, "Is this better?" This story is a school legend, and Roberta never has had to model a bad speech again!

Learning from the Past to Inform the Present

The presentation had been inspiring, and Roberta was wallowing in self-pity. At the conference we'd just attended, a teacher had led a session on his students' oral history project. They had researched an event that had occurred in their city seventy years earlier, interviewed elderly citizens who remembered it, and then served up wonderfully rich slices of that historical pie. The whole way home Roberta complained how lucky history teachers were. They had so many accessible troves of events to use for such exciting projects.

Then inspiration struck. The year was 1985, and the country was adither in anticipation of the return of Halley's Comet. Roberta put out an all-call to students and colleagues to bring in articles about the previous sightings of the famous comet, in 1910. She read aloud these articles describing people's recollections of the very visible and often frightening comet's tail that stretched across the sky. Student interest in these stories was high, so she offered extra credit to anyone who could locate and interview an elderly person who remembered the 1910 incident. The class brainstormed a list of the information they wanted to gather and turned it into a set of interview questions.

Students then wanted to know how to conduct an interview without a tape recorder. Roberta remembered how successfully students had used the research boxes for the animal report and suggested that they "box" their questions: if they filled in every box, they would know that they had answered all the questions. For the next two weeks (conveniently coinciding with Thanksgiving break, when visits with extended family were more likely), these young oral historians interviewed older relatives and visited nursing homes, gathering stories as they went.

Next Roberta revisited the stories in the articles she had gathered and discussed how the students might turn their raw data into narratives. She received sixteen written accounts from that class. These accounts were revised and edited, then published in a booklet entitled *Halley's Comet.* There were chronicles of sermons announcing the end of the world, rumors of blue men, and family viewings from the porch at four o'clock in the morning. Interviewees ranged from eighty-three to one-hundred-and-four years of age. The students who completed this extra-credit assignment came from all ability levels: EMR (educable mentally retarded), LD (learning disabled), ATP (academically talented), and regular (no labels) students contributed oral history accounts. Each was more exciting than the last.

The work of two students stands out. Sarah was extremely shy and withdrawn, so much so that she never ate lunch with other students. She turned in five interviews, obviously more comfortable talking with her grandmother and the other residents of a nearby nursing home. How good she must have felt about herself! Dennis had called his ninety-one-year-old great-grandfather for information and had interviewed him over the phone. By the time the *Halley's Comet* booklet was published for the class and earned its rightful place on The Cart and in the school library, his great-grandfather had died. Their conversation about Halley's Comet was the last time they spoke to each other.

Oral histories are wonderful ways for students to branch out beyond the confines of their times and lifestyles. They not only develop a deeper understanding of a particular era or event but also develop intergenerational understanding and appreciation. Oral histories can find a home in every subject, bridging conversations across generations and engendering mutual respect.

In addition to full-scale oral history projects, Roberta regularly prompts her students to interview other generations about the energy crisis of the seventies, early launches in the Mercury space program, the first moon landing in 1969, and the flu epidemic of 1918. Both of us have been interviewed by students in other classes about our recollections of President Kennedy's assassination, the Vietnam era, and what we eat for breakfast now versus when we were growing up. (We're always brought up short by the realization that today's teens think we're part of ancient history.)

Learning to Write Business Letters—In Science?

In the eighties, Roberta and her classes read an article from *Time* magazine that had been written five years earlier about the energy efficiency of the new Massachusetts Department of Transportation building in Boston. Students wanted to know if the new technologies had really worked. Roberta stifled the urge to say, "I'll find out and let you know"; instead, she posed the question, "How could we find out?" They quickly decided writing letters would be the best way but were not sure to whom the letters should go. Again, Roberta resisted the urge to jump in and tell them; instead, she listed their suggestions on the board—then-Governor Dukakis, the editor of *Time*, the Boston Chamber of Commerce, the Massachusetts Department of Transportation, the engineering firm that had designed the building, and the mayor of Boston. Together, they evaluated each source to determine who would be most likely to know and respond. They decided that the editor would not know, or he would have printed a follow-up story. Governor Dukakis and the mayor probably would just refer the letter to the Department of Transportation. That narrowed the choices to three: the Department of Transportation, the engineering firm, and the Chamber of Commerce. Volunteers drafted letters and brought them back to class the next day for feedback and approval. They also decided their letter would be taken more seriously if it were on school letterhead and looked like a business letter (a good reason to revisit the English book to check the format).

The real world met room 22 when the Chamber of Commerce did not respond to the letter and the Department of Transportation sent a booklet of rules and regulations concerning building use without any reference to their questions. However, the engineering firm saved the day. Karen, who had drafted and signed the letter to them (see Figure 11–3), was in the cafeteria eating lunch when Roberta found a large manila envelope addressed to Karen in her mailbox. Roberta ran to the cafeteria to deliver it. Karen, sitting with her friends, ripped it open to find a two-page letter and several articles on energy-efficient designs of buildings. With her classmates peering over her shoulder, she read the letter aloud, whooping with delight at the ending. A kind engineer had taken the time to write a personal note, asking Karen to remember to submit her résumé to the firm if she ultimately decided to enter the field of engineering! Today, Karen is married and a college graduate who did *not* become an engineer, but she mentions that letter whenever she bumps into Roberta on her visits home. What an impression real-life writing can make! This particular class became active letter writers, sending off missives to Congressmen and governmental agencies asking for information and expressing opinions. When a class video mentioned a building in Chicago that employed a number of energy-efficient features, they fired off another letter without prompting. (They never received a response but haunted the mailbox for months.)

Oxford Area Intermediate School
602 Garfield Street
Oxford, PA 19363
(215) 932-6615

Oxford Area School District

119 South Fifth Street • Oxford, Pa. 19363 • (215) 932-6600

March 30, 1989

Shooshanian Engineering Associates
330 Congress Street
Boston, MA 02210

Attention: Mr. Henry Eggert

Dear Sir:

Hello! My name is Karen Higgins. I attend Oxford Intermediate School, Oxford, Pennsylvania.

Our 8th Grade Science Class has just completed a unit on energy. We studied Nuclear, Solar and Electrical energy. We have discussed energy conservation and different possibilities of producing energy.

In one of our discussions, we read an article about the Transportation Building you designed in Boston. The article we read was from a Time Magazine dated January 9, 1984.

Our Science Class would like some updated information on the Transportation Building and would like to know if any other buildings or homes have been built following the same energy conservation principles.

Thank you in advance for your help. We appreciate any information you would send us as soon as possible.

Sincerely,

Karen B. Higgins
Oxford Intermediate School
602 Garfield Street
Oxford, PA 19363
c/o Mrs. Roberta McManus
(Science Teacher)

Figure 11–3. *Karen's letter*

Several years later, Roberta mentioned a news segment related to energy conservation that she had seen on *World News Tonight with Peter Jennings* the night before. Students wanted to know more, so Roberta moved into "business-letter mode." A group of students gave up their lunch and club periods to think through potential audiences and to draft, revise, and edit a letter (see Figure 11–4). When she read the opening line,

Oxford Area Intermediate School
602 Garfield Street
Oxford, PA 19363
(215) 932-6615

Oxford Area School District

119 South Fifth Street • Oxford, Pa, 19363 • (215) 932-6600

January 18, 1990

New England Power
Conservation and Land Management Section
25 Research Drive
Westboro, MA 01582

Dear Sir or Ms.:

We are inquring eighth-grade science students who are
interested in learning more information on your energy
conservation program which we were introduced to by ABC's
Peter Jennings on World News Tonight. We were fascinated by
the concept of home visitation to make homes in your service
area more energy efficient. We were especially interested
in the fluorescent bulbs that fit regular lamps and sockets.

We have prepared a list of questions and it would be
greatly appreciated if you would answer them. The questions
are:

 1. What is the number of houses you supply?
 2. Are most of your customers satisfied?
 3. What was the cost of the project compared to the
    cost of building a new power plant?
 4. Did you have to hire more people?
 5. How do we get these light bulbs?
 6. What gases are used in these bulbs?
 7. How long do the bulbs last?
 8. Why is the Philadelphia Electric Company not using
    this?
 9. Would you recommend this to other companies?
10. How much energy and money does the average
    homeowner save by using the new fouorescent
    bulbs?
11. What follow-ups are you using to keep energy
    levels down?

Please direct you response to the following address.

          Section 8-ST
          c/o Mrs. Mcmanus
          Oxford Intermediate School
          602 Garfield Street
          Oxford, PA 19363

Thank you for your time and consideration.

                    Sincerely,
                    Students of Section 8-ST

Figure 11–4. *Letter written by committee*

Roberta laughed. How many eighth graders speak like that? The young authors told her that they dressed up their vocabulary because they didn't want to appear "dumb" to the reader! Although their letter did not get a response, it inspired other students to do research of their own at local stores and to bring in articles that they found in magazines.

Letter writing has largely given way to the Internet. Today it is very common for students to e-mail from the classroom computer asking for updates on information and seeking responses to their questions. In addition, Roberta has turned the writing of invitations, announcements, and thank-you notes over to her students. Volunteers for this real-life writing are many, and the notion that they are writing to a real person for a real purpose makes students very conscientious!

Learning Beyond the Classroom

Roberta had one class of motivated high-energy students who loved challenges. She gave them one: design and develop an interesting, reusable way to help students understand how electricity is made. Meeting in groups, they brainstormed different ways of doing this. They knew from class lectures that three different types of electricity generating stations were within driving distance of the school: a fossil fuel-burning plant, a nuclear power plant, and a hydroelectric plant. The consensus of the groups was that visiting the experts at these three generating stations would give them the best information and that creating a video would capture their findings for posterity.

Harnessing their enthusiasm and channeling it into something doable was a challenge! Resisting the urge to organize the project for them, Roberta stayed on the sidelines as coach while they problem-solved how to get it all done. Students created and chose to work on one of five committees for the video: Introduction, Fossil Fuel, Nuclear Power, Hydroelectric Power, and Finale. Discussions were lively as they consulted diagrams of the generating stations and listed questions for the interviews. Using the mapping strategy that they had seen Roberta use so many times in class, each group fleshed out the qualities of good interviewers, then compared notes with the other groups. The groups revised their interview questions and elected the members who would represent the class at the three sites. Roberta found this democratic process interesting. Half the students chosen by peers would *not* have been those whom she would have picked using the typical-teacher screening tool of *is dependable, a hard worker, a good student, a leader*. However, she did not interfere. She was pleasantly surprised, and reminded once again of the importance of staying away from preconceived notions, when these students performed in stellar fashion.

Preproduction began in earnest. The three interviewers chosen to represent the class—and three cameramen (those whose parents allowed them to borrow the family camcorder!)—ate lunch in the science room day after day, practicing their interviewing skills on one another. On their own time, they subjected parents, friends, and anyone else who would listen to the same. Finally, the big day came. The students, the electric company representative who coordinated the trip, and Roberta set off on their one-hundred-mile circuit. Life lessons abounded that day. They learned that filming outdoors is problematic near an airport, in the wind, and next to a busy highway, and that simple interviews can last much longer than expected, necessitating schedule adjustments. They also learned that preparedness, good manners, and poise pay off. The managers of the generating plants were more than cooperative, taking time to explain their jobs and the science behind them to such a fine young audience. These young researchers had the opportunity to examine delivery systems, to wince at the noise of turbines, to explore control panels, and to marvel at the complexity of the systems they saw.

Returning to the school, their work continued. The "glamour" of being involved on-site was tempered by preparing an oral report to the class, briefing the Introduction Committee, and writing a set of scientific conclusions for the Finale Committee. Others were counting on them before they could do their jobs. In addition, there were thank-you letters to write to the experts who had taken time from their jobs to talk with them.

The Introduction and Finale Committees then prepared and taped their segments of the video. The young lady and gentleman who had been chosen as on-camera representatives arrived at school at 7:00 a.m. attired in a dress and make-up and a shirt and tie, respectively. After taping and before first period, they reverted to laid-back teen-agers, pulling shorts, sandals, and T-shirts out of their backpacks. School images are school images, after all!

A subcommittee undertook the task of creating the final product. Lacking editing equipment, they strung three TVs and VCRs together after school and combined the five separately filmed videotapes into one. In Hollywood style, they even tacked on outtakes at the end, room 22's very own "bloopers." What emerged may not have been polished enough for an Academy Award, but it accomplished its goal: a reusable way to help students understand how electricity is made. Its world premiere took place in all science classes in early June. Viewers responded to it in writing via three prompts: *The part I enjoyed the most was . . . , The part I still don't understand is . . . ,* and *My opinion of the video is . . .* Students' responses were overwhelming. Not only did they enjoy watching their classmates' production, they learned in the process. For the class that created the video, learning did not stop at the school door. Science came to life.

Learning to Inform the Public

STUDENTS: You want us to speak at a faculty meeting?

ROBERTA: It's your project. If you want this to work, it needs to come from you.

STUDENTS: But it's teachers! A room full of them! They won't want to hear from us.

ROBERTA: Why not? They don't know anything about this program and you do. You need to present it to them, and then present it to all of the students in the building.

STUDENTS: You'll speak, too. Right?

ROBERTA: No way. This is all yours.

And thus, Roberta and her environmental club known as Earth First launched the recycling program in their building. After writing letters to the school's head custodian and the district's business manager asking to schedule a meeting with them, the club members sat with the two men and learned about those blue boxes that suddenly had appeared in every classroom. They were intended for recycling, but the recycling campaign needed a jump-start. No one seemed to know what it was about, and informing them seemed to fit perfectly with the club's mission. Initially, they thought this would involve making posters and collecting paper. They never expected that they would have to become public speakers.

The old adage "practice makes perfect" was just what they needed to allay their fears. Whenever she has students speak in public, Roberta usually can recite everyone's speech without notes by the time they are finished with rehearsals. She suspects that the parents can, too. After much practice, Earth First members not only spoke to the faculty but also to the student body on three separate occasions to explain the program. The results? Their efforts and leadership met with such success that they were given an award by the county commissioners.

Success breeds confidence. Earth First began looking for another challenge. They had heard that a hands-on science Discovery Museum, previously set up and staffed by parents in one of the district's elementary schools, was in danger of being discontinued. With the sponsorship of Roberta and the elementary school's teacher of the academically talented, Lynda, the club reinvigorated the two-day science event for kindergartners and first graders. They gathered science equipment, hung posters, set up labs, and became the expert speakers and teachers for the younger children. They were surprised and flattered to find that the little ones treated them with the same awe and respect that they gave to the adults in the room. This opportunity to display their knowledge to an audience outside their peer group may have been a milestone in their growth. Currently, several of these former students are now pursuing science and education careers. Did it all start in middle school when they were given a chance to teach science to others? As real teachers, we really never know where our influence stops!

When Roberta's school became involved with Project ExCITE (Exploring the Integration of Technology and Education), her teaching duties expanded to include becoming project manager. This four-year endeavor, cosponsored by NASA and neighboring Lincoln University, brought many opportunities to expand science knowledge through technology. As you might expect, Roberta used it as a chance to support literacy skills as well. At an early stage in the project, she decided that students should do the majority of the presentations to their school and to the general public. Here was an opportunity to engage students in communicating with audiences around the world. Because her school was a two-year middle school, there was a recurring need to introduce the project to new students so they could go forth as ambassadors. Consequently, she was able to involve a large number of public-speaking "apprentices." With the technology brought forth by this project, she also was able to expand her students' presentation repertoires. Computer programs, scanners, digital cameras, and laser printers made elaborate display boards and Power Point slide shows possible.

Technology made it possible to "ratchet up" the presentations, but preparation is still preparation, and composition is still composition. The best technological bells and whistles will not mask a poorly conceived or inadequately developed speech. This was Roberta's strong message to these young presenters. Students worked in groups to decide topics and form subcommittees to do the hard work of preparation. They were astonished to find that a simple ten-minute speech accompanied by high-tech visual aids required hours of work. *Revise* became a common utterance as they wrote and refined their speeches and visuals. So did *practice* and *rehearse*. Feedback from peers was essential in these dry runs. *Poise, fluency,* and *preparedness* became watchwords. Often the presentations required both speakers and technology aides to coordinate their efforts to create a polished look. Due to the complexity of the project, most presentations required more than three student speakers.

In the course of the project, these middle schoolers made presentations to the student body, the school board, the Home and School Association, two local community groups, fellow middle school students in Pennsylvania and in California, on a TV news show, at the office of a U.S. Congressman, and at a local community celebration. They also took part in two distance learning presentations. In the process of honing science knowledge, they simultaneously learned how to work with others, how to speak confidently, how to use technology effectively, and how to budget time. After watching one of the presentations, Mallory's mother said to Roberta, "I just couldn't believe it when I saw my daughter up there! I'm so proud of her! You can use her any time you want for things like this!"

Learning to Interweave Curricula

The real world is not organized into separate blocks of knowledge. Only in schools do we find talk about literature scheduled to occur from 8:00–9:45, science from 9:48–10:27, social studies from 10:30–11:15. Calls for helping students make interdisciplinary connections are not new. As far back as John Dewey (1916, 1938), American education has been under scrutiny and, often, criticism for parceling out knowledge within separate disciplines. And the conversation still goes on. Our point is not to debate the issues surrounding discipline-specific versus interdisciplinary study but to share things that Roberta and her colleagues have found to be beneficial to their students.

When Roberta's principal began to talk with his teaching staff about the philosophical and practical differences between middle schools and junior high schools, he made strong arguments in favor of interdisciplinary studies. Intuitively, the argument fit with these teachers' experiences. They knew that students, especially at this age, looked to them to model creative thinking, problem solving, and teamwork. They also knew that students regarded them as representatives of separate bodies of knowledge who worked in isolation from one another. While they could see a bigger picture in which all that they taught was symbiotic with everything else, they knew that their students did not necessarily make the same connection.

Breaking out of an old mold is difficult, but Roberta and the other teachers on her team decided to test the waters with an interdisciplinary mini-unit on energy. This was an act of bravery on the part of the members of the team who were self-confessed science-phobes. Nevertheless, they took the plunge. Using a strategy that they employed with their students when they needed to help them make sense of new information, they developed a graphic organizer on which they listed the possible connections between energy and their subjects (see Figure 11–5). They surprised themselves with all the connections they could contribute. Coincidentally, at the same time the state of Pennsylvania was offering Governor's Energy Education Awards to students who completed a certain number of teacher-approved activities and projects. The team decided to challenge their students to earn enough points to earn the award. As a culmination of their efforts, the school designated two days as Energy Days. The pieces started to fit together.

During Energy Days, the team simply scrapped the regular schedule and created a new one with time frames that matched the energy activities (Figure 11–6). Some lasted twenty-five minutes while others took an entire hour. Here's what went on:

1. Guest speakers introduced students to careers and opportunities in the fields of solar and nuclear energy.
2. Students presented projects and speeches on energy issues that reflected their individual talents and interests. Some wrote short stories; those who had interviewed or administered surveys to adults summarized their findings.
3. Models of Drake's oil well, nuclear reactors, and solar houses filled tables.
4. Two young men displayed the newly learned soldering skills they had acquired as they connected solar cells to create a six-foot-by-three-foot panel that would power a car radio. (They almost dropped their project while carrying it outside. They had inadvertently left the radio on and were startled when music blared as they emerged from the building into the rays of the sun!)

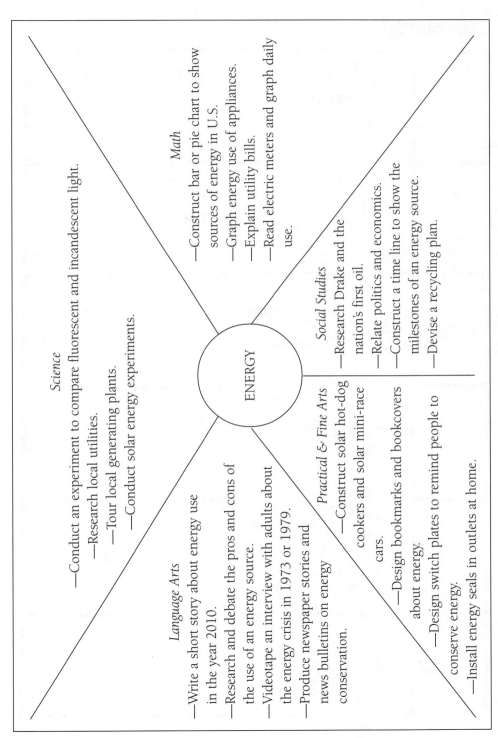

Figure 11–5. *Organizer for an interdisciplinary unit*

Period 1 room 16		Let the Sun Shine... Guest Speaker: Dr. Rand
Period 2 room 16		Write On! Use your pen to solve energy problems
Period 3 room 4		Video: A Can Do Attitude and Solar Power
Period 4 cafeteria		P.R.I.S.E. - Predicting Results in Solar Experiments
Period 5 room 22		It's Show Time! Student Speeches
Period 7 room 25		Continue Building for the Future

Figure 11–6. *Sample of one day's schedule*

5. Having spent several days researching the safety of nuclear power plants in language arts class, students participated in a judged debate entitled "To Nuke or Not to Nuke—That Is the Question." Following the rules of a debate proved difficult for the students as their differences in opinion became apparent. The debate escalated in excitement and volume.

6. Math teachers presented energy information and students divided into groups to devise ways to interpret those figures graphically.

7. In social studies classes, students applied their map skills to represent energy sources geographically.

8. Art students made conservation reminders to post around the school and in their homes. They also "rebuilt" a city whose energy sources had been "destroyed" in a flood, creating a city that conformed to their visions and opinions of energy use.

9. Science students conducted experiments on energy transformations and solar power.

10. Industrial arts students made solar hot-dog cookers, and, in front of the entire team of students, brave Principal Bob ate a solar-cooked lunch consisting of hot dogs, tea, and an apple snack. (Clearly, the man had a cast-iron stomach.)

The two days concluded with an inspiring video showing the achievements of college students who used cutting-edge technology and had "can do" attitudes.

An overall assessment of this interdisciplinary unit yielded a resounding "thumbs up." Students welcomed the opportunity to develop expertise in a field of study. In the two years of this project in conjunction with the Governor's Award, 88 percent of the eligible students won the award in the first year, an impressive 91 percent the second. More important, pupils learned critical lessons about goal setting, time management, and cooperation that will carry over into their lifetimes.

Learning Through the Arts

> The intuitive mind is a sacred gift and the rational mind is a faithful servant. We have created a society that honors the servant and has forgotten the gift.
>
> —Albert Einstein

We can't say it better than that. Research on multiple intelligences (Gardner 1993) and learning styles (Gregorc 1986; McCarthy 2000) has shown that human intellect reflects much more than the rational knowledge historically taught in school. Without a doubt, there is much rationality in science, but even in a subject traditionally thought to be so overwhelmingly rational, the intuitive mind can be stimulated by the arts. For some students the arts are a conduit through which the rational mind can travel. For some, being able to express themselves and what they know through artistic representation is a way they can shine in a school situation that traditionally has valued the more rational mind. For others, it is a stretch, but one that they need to make.

To paraphrase former president Ronald Reagan, we believe that the humanities are humanizing and the liberal arts liberating. During any half-hour TV show, pay attention to the commercials. If you came from outer space and wanted to know what Earthlings are like, you would think we are one sick bunch. We have aching muscles, respiratory distress, anxiety, depression, bad backs, headaches, sore feet, digestive problems galore, memory loss, and assorted dysfunctions we can't mention in a nice book. Our humanity is stressed, and our senses of well-being unliberated. We make no claims to be art, music, or drama therapists, but people in those professions seem to understand what we intuitively feel: the arts help people live more fully. So we say, "Bring on the arts!"

Problem Solving the Rube Goldberg Way

If balance between the intuitive and the rational, the arts and sciences, is what we desire, then artist and engineer Reuben Lucius Goldberg is a science teacher's dream. His Pulitzer Prize-winning "Invention" cartoons, depicting complex ways of completing simple tasks, brought the label "Rube Goldberg machine" into the American lexicon. He drew his cartoons to satirize the technology and gadgetry of the early part of the twentieth century, and we can only wonder what he would think about today! Purdue University holds the National Rube Goldberg Machine Contest annually, in which teams are given a simple problem—putting toothpaste on a toothbrush, for example—for which they must develop the most convoluted and complex solution they can. The more steps, the better! The exercise pulls them away from conventional problem-solving strategies and forces them into their imagination and intuition.

Roberta always shares Goldberg's humorous inventions with her classes when they study simple machines. They recall the Goldberg-esque game of their youths, Mousetrap, enjoy looking at Roberta's collection of his cartoons, and visit the website <www.rubegoldberg.com>. She doesn't have enough time for students to create a Rube Goldberg project, Purdue-style. They do have time, however, to draw one in the cartoon style of Goldberg. This project is always one of their favorites of the year. The simple problem Roberta tells them to solve relates to their classroom. Over the last ten years, she has posed these situations:

1. Take a pencil out of a box, sharpen it, and write Mrs. McManus a message.
2. Uncap an alcohol burner, unscrew the lid, fill the burner with alcohol, screw the lid back on, put the burner under a ring stand, and light the burner.
3. Load a tape into a VCR, turn on the VCR and the TV, and watch a science video.

4. Collect a set of numbered textbooks in the proper sequence and return them to the bookcase.

5. Collate eight copies of eight different pages, punch holes in them, staple each set, and stack in one pile.

6. Put fifteen lab kits into their proper spot on two shelves of a moving cart. Return the cart to the front of the classroom.

7. Put up all thirty chairs in the classroom onto the lab tables.

8. Use a cleanser and scrub one row of lab tables.

9. Lift the wood cover from the fish tank, pick up the can of fish food, shake the can, put it down, and return the lid to the top of the tank.

10. Erase and wash the blackboard, leaving no puddles.

In keeping with Goldberg's style, they must use simple machines (pulleys, screws, inclined planes, wheel and axle, levers, and wedges), common household items, and other products of their imaginations. They can choose to work in pairs, groups of three, or alone to create not only the drawing but a legend identifying all the simple machines used, a story map to explain the sequence of events, and finally, a presentation to their classmates. After Roberta reviews appropriate behavior for choosing and working with partners and shares the grading rubric, they all adjourn to the cafeteria, where they can spread out and work. She loves to watch them share their ideas. They become quite animated, using their hands to demonstrate the work of the simple machines they are considering, and fill the room with an industrious, on-task hum of activity.

Although the problem to be solved is limited to something that occurs in the classroom, the events depicted can take place outside the classroom. Students have included bathtubs, trampolines, marbles, dogs who bite hot chili peppers, and rocking grandmas. Talented animals frequently figure into the events; cows, mice, birds, and especially frogs appear regularly. Roberta laughed when her messy desk (complete with student work marked with As) and her head atop Cindy Crawford's body cut from a magazine layout appeared in a student's Goldberg project. Sometimes they draw her wearing clothing that she recognizes from her wardrobe, but she had to tell one group that she does *not* wear combat boots with skirts!

They think they're just having fun, but we know differently. In order to complete this project, they have to *know* their science. They have to exercise their faithful-servant rational mind as well as their sacred-gift intuitive mind. Under Roberta's watchful eye, they exercise all ten qualities sought by the Fortune 500 companies. This assignment is a great improvement over just another list or analysis of simple machines.

Music and Drama

The Earth First club wanted to celebrate Earth Day in a special way. To call attention to this day, they decided to create a slide show set to music, so they brought in an assortment of musical choices—soft rock, country, hard rock, and easy listening. One group of girls lobbied heavily for the song "From a Distance" (Jackson and Traywick n.d.), bringing a copy of the lyrics with them to make their point. Their preference prevailed, and students set about looking for pictures to match the words of the song. With the expert advice and equipment of technology educator Bob, they converted pictures from magazines into slides. Soon Roberta's classroom looked like a massive art project run amok, as magazines and clippings spilled off of the counters onto the floor. The room became a frenzy of layouts and photo shoots—and students loved using the lingo of fashion photographers. Each phrase in the song had a corresponding slide—images of lighthouses, heaps of garbage, autumnal foliage, soaring eagles, fields of daisies, cute animals, little children, ocean waves crashing onshore, and a view of Earth from space. As they struggled to match the slides to the music, they began to sing along. Needless to say, the lyrics were etched into everyone's brain by the time the show was complete.

Students were so pleased with their final product that they asked to be able to develop an Earth Day assembly for the student body to showcase it. Roberta gave her approval and secured the necessary permission but told them it was their show. She would not even appear on stage. With a new goal in sight, the club decided that short skits would be just the things to enhance the slide show and formed committees to develop them. Roberta began as a cheerleader, encouraging them. Before long, however, that role changed to *nag*. This group had trouble keeping pace with the project, and she had to stop and "read them the riot act." They missed their April Earth Day deadline, and Roberta was becoming convinced that they wouldn't finish it by their high school graduations. Finally they pulled it together and it was wonderful, restoring her faith in projects like this. (Real teachers, you know the feeling.) They put in long hours out of school writing, rehearsing, and refining their skits. Sketches included past and future newsbreaks, a Star Trek episode, game shows, a scene in a doctor's office, and political commentary. They gave two performances in their own building, then went to one of the elementary schools and wowed that audience, too. They more than fulfilled their goal.

The next year, the returning nucleus of the Earth First club who had not moved on to the high school decided to reuse the slide show, but prepare new skits centered around the theme of "a day of TV." Remembering the problems the year before, they advised the younger members of the club about budgeting their time, and this time they were able to meet their Earth Day deadline in April. Their skits included takeoffs on morning and evening news shows, game shows, soap operas, talk shows, commercials, and a parody of David Letterman's top ten list. Their sense of accomplishment and thrill over their end products was one of those intangible rewards that keep good teachers teaching. The angst of the previous year came into perspective when Roberta saw how the older students had grown because of it and how they handled themselves well as models for the younger ones. Real teachers know that gratification is something we sometimes have to wait for.

Art to Learn

Safety is of paramount concern in lab-oriented science classes, and eighth graders don't always realize the potential dangers. To raise consciousness, Roberta and fellow science teacher Al wrote a Lab Safety Guide for students that both they and their parents must sign. In addition to that, they spent much class time reinforcing lab rules and regulations. Still, it didn't seem enough. The logical and rational seemed to meet glazed-over expressions; the students just wanted to get on with doing the labs. Roberta and Al wondered if the creative and intuitive might be the inroad they needed. So, they gave each student the assignment to create a miniposter, nine by twelve inches in size, to illustrate one of the safety rules. The resulting posters were amazing. Using computer-generated layouts, hand-drawn illustrations, magazine cutouts, photos, glitter, construction paper, and always at least one with glued-on pasta, they wowed their teachers with their ingenuity. Each year, the current group of students hangs its posters in the hallway outside the science rooms. Each year, the younger students get to enjoy not only the art but also an advance "heads-up" about lab safety to come.

Roberta and colleague Jen give their seventh graders a chance to show off their creative sides with cell-analogy posters. Through analogical thinking, this assignment helps students draw comparisons between the cell, unseeable to the naked eye, and the concrete objects in their lives that serve similar functions. For example, a picture of an orchestra conductor with a line connecting it to the nucleus of a cell yields this analogy: *The nucleus controls the activities of a cell just as this conductor controls the activities of his orchestra.* Pictures of coaches and quarterbacks cut from sports magazines fit this analogy well, too. Glued-on trash bags and pictures of commodes often represent vacuoles. As students develop these real-life analogies, they deepen their understanding of the science of cells. Roberta knew that Sarah really understood mitochondria when she glued on a picture of her little brother playing baseball and drew the analogy that just as her little brother is the most energetic member of her family, the mitochondria is the powerhouse of the cell!

Shaping Lifetimes

Education for a lifetime, and education that is lifelike: we don't believe this has to be a contradiction of terms. It does, however, require us to step beyond our preoccupations with content to think of broader processes and habits of mind. The reward for this is great, stemming far beyond contract talks and paychecks. We all can remember the guidance of particular teachers from our past whose lessons we still carry in our head today as we continue to learn. As real teachers, we know the thrill of having a former student come back to us years later and tell us how much we affected their thinking. Nothing rivals the sense of knowing that what we do changes people's lives. Real teachers, *how* we teach really does shape the future.

CHAPTER 12

LIFELONG TEACHING

This thing we do called teaching is not a passing phase. We are teachers for a lifetime. Because we teach, we feel compelled to keep learning and growing. If *we* were to become bored with what we do, *our students* would become bored with what we do. So we keep on adding to our teaching repertoires, concurring with Joyce and Weil that "as teachers increase their repertoires, so will students increase *theirs* and become more powerful and multifaceted learners" (1986, 22). It's a ripple effect, and it keeps all of us on our toes.

Roberta: My Continuing Journey as a Middle School Science Teacher

This summer I played a role in hiring an additional science teacher in my building. Denise, who eventually got the job, said in her interview, "My teaching style is still evolving." She said it in a very quiet, almost apologetic way, letting us know that although she had some teaching experience, she wasn't a finished product and still had a lot to learn. The mother in me wanted to lean over and pat her hand, telling her it was okay. The professional in me wanted to shout, "Right on!" My teaching style is still evolving too, and it had better continue to evolve! Changes in society, in educational research, and state regulations dictate it. More important, concern for what is best for my students makes me strive continually to do better. If my style stops evolving, if I stop learning, or if I become complacent in my daily work, then it's time for me to leave, to start another career or take early retirement.

Teachers need to keep learning. That means constantly trying new methods or giving our students new experiences. We need to stay current, and that's not always easy. In 1996, principal Bob wrote in a staff newsletter:

> As I see it, the most important quality you can have as a teacher is the ability to be a reflective practitioner. . . . Daily reflection plays a vital role in your success as a classroom teacher. However, remember that reflection is only one piece of the puzzle. If reflection is

to be effective, it must be followed by change or it becomes simply wishful thinking. Life is not stagnant, and our classrooms should not be either. (Farr 1996)

Always Evolving, Ever Learning

Frankly, my job today is harder than when I began teaching. Teachers now are responsible for so much more than just our content. The list of innovations in Chapter 2 is just an example. We are blamed for many of society's problems and for the rising tax rates within our communities. Politicians belittle public education, seemingly bent on undoing the very system within which we work. On one hand, it is easy to understand why teachers succumb to burnout or why they simply hunker down and ride out the storms that blow around them, content to stagnate through cycle after cycle. On the other, we defeat ourselves and, more important, our students if we do so. My solution has been to keep renewing myself through lifelong learning.

If I am enthusiastic about learning new things, I pass that enthusiasm on to my students. If I am stretching myself to the maximum of my learning curve, I can better empathize with young learners. For example, the last several courses I have taken have been about using computers. There is an old Amish saying in our area, *The hurrier I go, the behinder I get*. The more courses I take, the more technologically behind I feel. "Get used to it!" I tell myself. I've had to accept that I will not be the most knowledgeable one in the room. This is good for me. We teachers need to keep in contact with the part of us that doesn't know it all, that isn't the sage on the stage, that isn't the first one in the group to "get it." It makes us more understanding and, we hope, more patient with our students who experience this same feeling.

What I *am* good at, however, is asking for help. My students delight in helping me learn about computers, sharing the expertise that seems to come so easily to their generation. I tell them that there are many thirteen-year-olds who know far more than I do about technology, and this thrills them. (I've even been known to play dumber than I am in order to draw students into a lesson.) When they see me sharing my struggles to stay current and my willingness to learn and to ask for help, they see a model of adult learning. When they hear me call out to colleagues Al and Bob for help, they see that cooperation and collaboration are part of what adults *do* in real life. They see that people function within communities of learners.

Part of my evolution as a teacher has been to learn that I am a *researcher* of my own practice. It is so easy to abdicate that role. While grocery shopping this summer, I ran into fellow teacher Debbie, who inquired about the progress of this book. Then she asked, "How do you do your research? On the Internet?" I answered, "Oh, Donna knows all that and provides the theory references." On the way home, I realized that was only half an answer. I had lapsed into my traditional teacher mindset of research being something *other people* do. *I* am a researcher. I conduct research every day in room 22 every year I teach. Why are we teachers so quick to discredit our own knowledge gained through daily contact with our students? We need to start listening more to our own voice and share our work. In my classroom, I constantly ask students how they feel about their learning and about my teaching style, through discussions and anonymous questionnaires. Then I choose my course of action. I have changed a unit's pace, a project's requirements, and the manner in which we read based on my thinking about what my students have told me. My curriculum and pedagogy are much stronger for having researched my practice.

Reading and Writing in the Content Areas Works!

About ten years ago I attended an educational conference about implementing ways to increase students' abilities to read, write, and talk across the curriculum. We spent most of the morning listening to speakers and then divided into groups based on the grade levels and subjects we taught. Contrasted with the large number of elementary and secondary English teachers, there were just five of us representing the content areas—two science teachers, one social studies teacher, and two math and science professors who assigned student teacher placements. The science professor opened our discussion by saying, "Reading? Writing? Science?—Horse Manure!" (Actually, he used an earthier term.) My jaw hit the floor. But I'd heard comments like his before. He assumed that reading, writing, and talking were the responsibilities of the English/language arts teachers, not ours. He assumed his students would be able to transfer those skills to his classroom, and he sent his student teachers out with the same mindset.

I can back up my contention that *every* teacher should guide reading, writing, listening, and speaking in their content-area classes. *It works*: I have proof from my own classroom. As you learned in Chapter 1, I began to infuse reading and writing strategies into my teaching because I was frustrated with my failure rate. For the first five years of teaching, I failed, on average, fifteen students a year. During the first year I worked with Donna and the Building Leadership Team to reconceptualize my teaching, that number dropped to five and has never reached that high again. As I have increased the support I provide for learning, there have been five years in which every student has passed my class. Do I have small class sizes? No. I teach between 120 and 160 students a year. Am I an easy teacher? No. I am known to cover material in depth and to have high standards.

I take my low failure rate as an indication that my becoming a *teacher of process* as well as a *teacher of content* made me a better teacher. As an added benefit, my discipline problems *decreased* as my students' confidence in learning *increased*. We are a community of learners in my classes, helping one another grasp the processes we need to do the learning we must. Within this sense of community, everyone seems to behave better and try harder. Of the approximately 1,450 students I have taught in the past ten years, I have only had to send three to the office because of discipline problems. And I don't teach angels! Their success in learning seems to breed respect—for themselves, for me, and for the others in the class. To behave badly would be letting themselves and the rest of us down.

Not Going It Alone

My journey has been one of constant change. I've tried many new things. However, these changes and improvements have not happened in a vacuum. I'm blessed to have colleagues who recognize that two heads are better than one. We collaborate. As we change our curriculum to meet our new state standards, as we adjust to new methods of evaluation, and as we incorporate more and more standardized tests into our work, we act together. And not just on inservice days or during prep days in the summer. We work together, collaborate, and share as a part of daily life. Our science teachers do not need assigned department meetings to bring us together. We talk and share ideas every day. A new computer program, video, or lab to try out? A new project to create? We do it together after school. We meet in the hallways between classes to share what worked and what didn't. We create, work, and reflect together. This enriches us, and we constantly tell each other, "I couldn't do this without you." Al, Jen, and I make a good team that has been able to welcome newcomer Amanda into our shared collaboration. Beyond my department, I find many collaborators among the rest of the faculty. When the going gets tough, these are the people I run to. Collaboration is invaluable to me because of the benefits it bestows on my students. I cannot imagine working in isolation.

The collaboration that has made by far the biggest impact on me has been with Donna, my coauthor. In a speech over twelve years ago, I credited her with improving my teaching because she was "pushy." I still think that she's pushy—in a nice way. She pushes me to try new things, to take risks, and to be a better teacher. (And I don't always resist for two years as I did with writing!) We all need friends like Donna to push us to enrich ourselves as educators and as people. She keeps me current on the latest developments in education by reading widely, consolidating the information into something I can use, and directing me toward articles and books that specifically relate to me. This frees me to continue my reading in the ever-changing field of science. Donna presents me with theory and challenges me to put it into practical use in my classes.

It's late now, and I need to get to bed. Tomorrow another school year begins, with a new group of students. My journey continues. . . .

Donna: My Continuing Journey as a Literacy Professor and Researcher

Over my years no longer spent in a K–12 classroom, I have developed an intense respect for the teachers who provide America's compulsory education. I hope I never lose it. These people shape every one of our future citizens. In no way am I demeaning what

I did as an administrator or what I do now as a university professor. But the real work of educating three-to-eighteen-year-olds—whether and how well it gets done—is in the hands of our public and private school teachers.

I'll say it point blank. Teaching first grade in a public school was by far the most difficult work I've ever done. My job now is not easy. The pressure to teach well, to publish or perish, and to serve on committess and task forces is very real. My colleagues and I talk about it outside our office doors regularly. Office doors. Funny. Real K–12 teachers don't have office doors. They don't have offices. Or phones. They can't go to the restroom unless it's a prep period. Teaching in basic education is hard. I say all this because we who are not there, or who have left that life, sometimes tend to forget, to exhibit selective amnesia, or even to become pompous, caught up in our own agendas and the way it *oughta* be.

Different Facets, Same Prism

None of us is better or more important than the other. We are just different facets of the same complex prism—providing the best possible education to young people. In each of our respective positions, we have unique opportunities to inform the business of teaching and learning. I tell my graduate students that I learn as much from them as they do from me, and I mean it. That's the way it should be. As a professor, my ideas for teaching may have potential, but they are only good if someone can, and does, use them. Many times, Roberta has taken an idea of mine that I have grounded in theory and run with it, not doing it exactly the way I conceived it but tempering it to make it fit her classroom. After synthesizing some of what we know about how students learn, I'll often say to Roberta, "Hey, I've got this great idea that I think will work. Want to try it out?" After trying out an idea, she'll often say, "Great idea, but I had to change it because . . . ," adding her own layer of reality. And it's not uncommon for Roberta, after discovering an activity that really works for her students, to call me to find out the likely theoretical reasons. My theory informs her practice, and her practice informs my theory. We are doing different aspects of the same job: making meaning out of this business of teaching and learning. Every professor needs a trusted basic education buddy, and every K–12 teacher needs a trusted professor buddy. We keep each other honest.

As an education professor, I am expected to maintain a scholarly agenda—to do the research and to write. The facet of the prism that I represent gives me the time and mandate to tell the stories of education. But I am more and more convinced that classroom teachers have the real stories, the ones worth telling. When Roberta and I write together, we share our respective areas of expertise. Her classroom stories are vibrant, but she defers to me for what she calls "the theory, the names, the labels, and fixing the adverbs and stuff." She tells the stories; I fold them into a manuscript. Her job gives her the time and place in which the stories happen; mine gives me the time and place to connect them and write them down.

Releasing the Silenced Teacher Voice

As a professor, I look for opportunities to help teachers tell their stories in their own voices. Rather than assigning research papers that ask graduate students to rehash other people's thoughts, I like to ask them to speak about their own experiences. In my classes, they have written literacy autobiographies comparing and contrasting their own reading and writing history with current pedagogy, and they have written richly detailed vignettes about real situations in their classroom. They have written midterm reflections about links they are forging between their classroom and the course readings, final reflections entitled *I Used to Think . . . but [and] Now I Know . . .* , and visionary pieces about how they can weave new understanding into their teaching. I want them to take from my courses a newfound sense of their own voice in the field.

My colleague Sandy Hoffman and I have engaged our graduate students in teacher-research for many years (Hoffman and Topping 1999; Topping and Hoffman [forthcoming 2002]). We firmly believe that their "systematic and intentional inquiry into practice" (Cochran-Smith and Lytle 1993, 27) is a critical addition to the body of knowledge about education. Their teacher voices have been emboldened in our classes when they realize that we think they have important things to say. We see their consciousness crest as they begin to view themselves as researchers.

But beyond our graduate classes what happens? Just recently we surveyed our former students about the teacher-research studies they did with us and their ongoing teacher-research (Topping and Hoffman, in progress). Sadly, we found that most of them have not continued to conduct formal teacher-research studies. Why? Three factors come into play.

First, teachers cited the archenemy, *time*, as a major deterrent. Simply, their energies are sapped by teaching. The infrastructure of real schools is such that their would-be scholarly agendas are trumped by getting through each day.

A second factor reinforces the first. They feel that *no one listens*. For the most part they find that in their real world of school, they are not recognized as a voice of authority in the field. Or if they are, their knowledge is relegated to the status of teacher *lore* (North 1987). The prevailing opinion of many in their world is that *others*—-with more degrees, more credentials, or more name-recognition—deserve the title of "authority." Already exhausted by teaching, they question why they should bother to research and write when nobody listens.

A third factor insidiously plays into this reluctance as well. Not long ago I attended a meeting at which I was one of a very few professors; most of the attendees were teachers and administrators in the public schools. The topic of the day was standardized assessments. The stories told around my table were rich, the level of insight high— about this or that particular assessment and about student assessment in general. As we talked and these real teachers and administrators' stories came out, I kept urging them to speak up in the larger meeting, to voice objections and raise points based on real school experience. They wouldn't. They feared repercussions, that their comments would get back to their districts. Bolstered by the academic freedom clause in my professor's contract that (thankfully) allows those of us in higher education to tell what we see as the truth, I wrote their comments and questions down on the "question" cards we were given. The session moderator subsequently read them aloud to the entire assembly in a tone clearly derisive of anyone who would have written such things. At that meeting, there was a single accepted point of view; anyone not subscribing to it was an outcast. It is no wonder that teachers maintain their silence when they feel they *can't* tell their stories honestly.

Whether we feel we deserve the honor or not, people historically have listened to those of us whose title is professor or researcher. They have looked to *us* for knowledge. Therefore, it is imperative that I find ways to let real teachers' stories be told. The collaborative research and writing that Roberta and I do is one way. Valuing teachers and encouraging them to believe in *themselves* as researchers and writers is another. Incorporating activities into my classes that enable teachers to find their voice as a writer is at the core of how I teach. Until teachers feel there is time, an audience, and the freedom for them to tell their stories on their own, we professors need to help them do it, or their voices will be silenced for sure.

Be Real People First

As I was writing this, I received an e-mail from Roberta containing a draft of another section of this book. She also gloated that she had just bought an antique Hoosier cabinet for $350. I e-mailed back with one of my section drafts, preceding it with the rebuke, "You should be in jail for robbery—$350 is a steal!" Yes, this book is important. What we do professionally is important. But enjoying the pleasures of life with family and friends is more so. We are better educators because we have rich lives outside our school buildings. Every one of Roberta's and my writing sessions begins with an update on what our families are doing, of our latest antiquing "finds," and what's happening to whom among our mutual acquaintances. We also laugh a lot about how differently we approach tasks and congratulate ourselves on how we complement each other in the ways in which we process information. Our styles are different, but we enjoy celebrating these differences that stretch us.

Life is to be learned from. We need to stay open to everything, have a perpetual to-do list. We need to make sure there is always something to look forward to. My Aunt Barbara, age eighty-nine, diabetic, bedfast in a nursing home, and almost blind, called recently with some news. Her doctor had just told her that she might be a candidate for eye surgery that would restore at least some of her vision. She was terribly excited— she wants to learn to use the computer and this would mean she could! That's who I want to be—active, vital, and soaking up life until there is no more. To be real teachers, we have to be real people first.

And now I have to figure out what to fix for dinner and see what the kids are up to.

The Ongoing Collaborative Journey

Our collaboration is unique. We bring our respective backgrounds in science and literacy, public school and the university, together in a way that energizes us both. As the summer of book writing came to an end and a new school year approached, we kept interrupting our writing to talk about new things we wanted to try this year in our classes. One idea seemed to spring off another. An idea would surface, submerge and be bathed and rebathed in theory, resurface in a new form, and then be cast to suit either middle school or university students. This interplay of ideas—practice to theory to practice—is exciting and has kept us passionate about what we do. We wish every teacher this type of collaboration, which Roberta's colleague Jen summarizes so well:

> Collaborating gives me confidence to develop my own ideas and reduces the stress of having to do it by myself. I feel free to bounce ideas back and forth and know that together we'll produce something far more creative than I could have done alone.

Getting started is sometimes the hardest part. Our advice to those wishing to rethink their teaching is, "Choose one thing." Choose the one thing in each unit that your students have the most trouble learning—that is the hardest to teach—that you dread the most—and try one of the ideas you've read about in this book. If you are just starting out, think about your lessons in terms of *before, during,* and *after.* Choose one part of that sequence and try an idea you've heard about. Watch student reactions as you teach, and ask them to tell you what worked for them and what didn't. Keep a pad of sticky notes beside you as you teach, and make notes about the "one thing" you will need to fix the next time you teach this unit. Before long, all the "one things" you have chosen will add up to a lot of things that make teaching and learning successful.

Our shared hope is that our efforts and stories will help you and your collaborators increase your personal repertoires of teaching strategies. And with that, we bid you a successful journey.

Science 7   Scholar _____

SURVEYING YOUR TEXTBOOK

1. What is the book's title?

   _____

2. How many pages are in the book?

   _____

3. Was the book written or revised recently? _____

   Why might this make a difference? _____

   _____

   _____

4. Examine the table of contents to see if it is helpful. Use it to answer the following.

   Can you use the table of contents to   If yes, on
   find the following information?   what page is it?

	yes or no?	
microscope parts		
cell structure		
conifers		
fission		
George Washington Carver		

5. Look at Chapter 3 on pages 41–61.

Are there chapter headings? _____ How many? _____

Are there subheadings? _____ How many? _____

List the other *TYPES* of *organization* found between pages 41 and 58. (DO NOT give specific titles.) Hint: There are 9 answers. You are to list 5 of them.

a.

b.

c.

d.

e.

6. Are there pictures in this chapter? _____

Are there maps in this chapter? _____

Are there charts in this chapter? _____

7. Does this chapter have a summary? _____

8. What two types of activities does this book suggest to *further* your understanding of each chapter? Hint: Look at page 61.

a.

b.

9. This book has a glossary. Where is it? _____

What kind of information does a glossary give?

10. How many appendixes does this book have? _____

Where are they located? _____

11. Where is the index in this book? _____

Put a check mark beside the information that you can find using your index.

_____ microsope parts   _____ conifers
_____ cell structure   _____ fission
_____ amphibians   _____ George Washington Carver

Compare these answers to those in number 4.

12. Examine the table of contents again. Next, write 3 or 4 sentences summarizing the organizational plan of the book.

Science 7   Cytologist _____
Reading Guide: Cells and Structure
Reference: Life Science, pages 47–54

CELLS & STRUCTURE

1. You have probably heard about cells in science class last year. *BEFORE* you
   start to read, write three *complete* sentences about cells.

   a. _____

   b. _____

   c. _____

2. The "Cells and Structure" section in your book is divided into three subheadings. Please list them.

   a. _____

   b. _____

   c. _____

****REMINDER**** Use the SQ3R study plan as you read these pages. Be especially sure to *read* the questions *BEFORE* you read each section.

Cell Theory pages 47–48

3. Using the first paragraph of this section, give a definition of a cell.

   _____

4. Why do we use microscopes to study cells? _____

5. Name the scientist who first saw cells. _____

6. List two ideas in "Cell Theory," found in the top paragraph of page 48.

   a. _____

   b. _____

Cell Structure page 48–49

7. Do all cells have cell membranes? _____

8. Name two jobs of cell membranes.

   a. _____

   b. _____

9. Cell membranes are made of _____ and _____ .

10. Put a check mark in front of all the statements that are TRUE. (Leave the false statements blank!)

   _____ a. The nucleus carries the code that controls cell activities.

   _____ b. The nucleus is usually found near the center of a cell.

   _____ c. A nucleus is found in every cell.

   _____ d. Chromosomes are found in the nucleus.

11. What is cytoplasm? _____

   _____

12. Name two things that can be found in cytoplasm.

   a. _____   b. _____

13. Name two types of cells without a nucleus.

   a. _____   b. _____

14. Define cell wall. _____

   _____

15. How is a cell wall like the wall of a building? _____

   _____

16. Do you have cell walls in your bone cells? _____

Career page 49

17. List two jobs of a cytotechnologist?

   a. _____

   b. _____

Cell Parts pages 51–54

18. Matching—give the letter of the best answer.

    _____ powerhouse of the cell

    _____ contain chlorophyll

    _____ tubes to connect nucleus to membrane

    _____ make protein

    _____ sac to hold water & food

    a. endoplasmic reticulum
    b. ribosomes
    c. mitochodria
    d. vacuole
    e. chloroplasts

19. What is the job of Golgi bodies? _____

20. Compare the drawings on page 52. Name two cell parts found in plant cells ONLY.

    a. _____ b. _____

21. Fill in the following chart.

cell part	function
nucleus	
cell membrane	
cell wall	
chloroplast	
vacuole	
cytoplasm	

22. Look back to the sentences you wrote for number 1. Would you find it easy to write three more sentences about cells? Try it!

    a. _____

    b. _____

    c. _____

Name _____

REVIEW CIRCLES

_____   _____

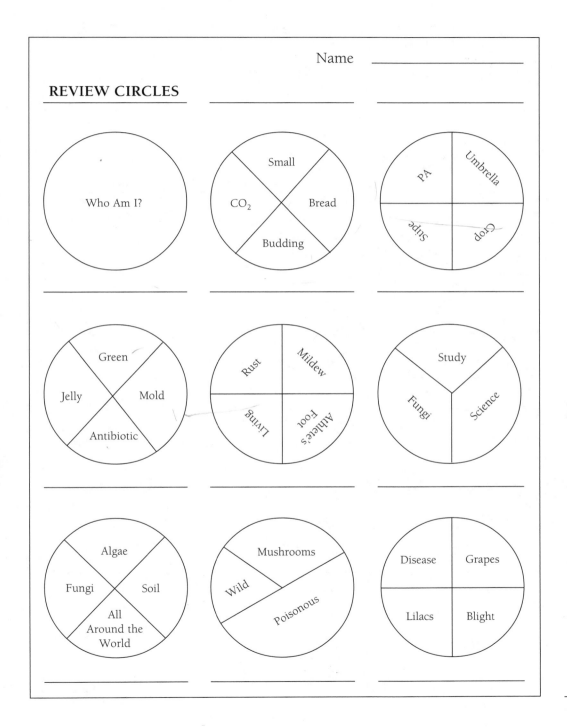

Circle 1: Who Am I?

Circle 2: Small, CO$_2$, Bread, Budding

Circle 3: PA, Umbrella, Stipe, Crop

Circle 4: Green, Jelly, Mold, Antibiotic

Circle 5: Rust, Mildew, Living, Athlete's Foot

Circle 6: Study, Fungi, Science

Circle 7: Algae, Fungi, Soil, All Around the World

Circle 8: Mushrooms, Wild, Poisonous

Circle 9: Disease, Grapes, Lilacs, Blight

_____   _____   _____

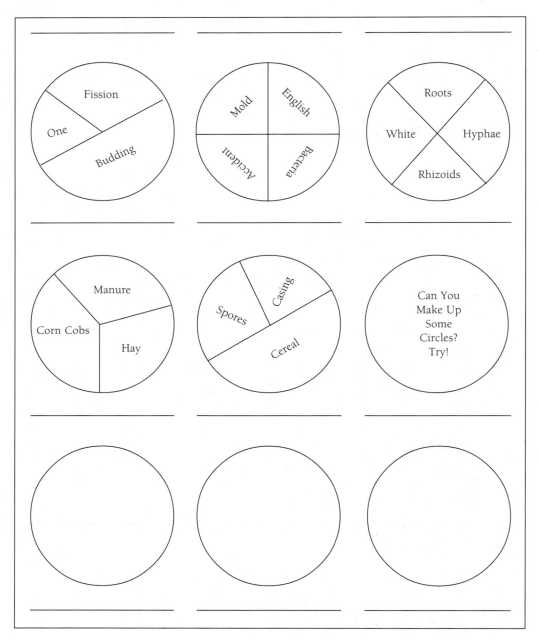

Science 7: Review   Pathologist _____
                                     Section   _____

REVIEW—A, B, C . . . SIMPLE!

The rules are simple. You have been assigned to a particular section. Tomorrow in class, you will have an opportunity to compare your answers with another person assigned to your same section. After this "double-check," you will team up with someone from each of the other sections to copy/learn/teach from one another. (Failure to do your homework means you will do ALL of the sections on your own. It's your choice!)

DIRECTIONS—The beginning letter of the answer is given for you—you provide the answer. Use your notebook and textbook as resources.

A_____   1. disease caused by HIV that has reached epidemic stages

_____   2. penicillin was the first

_____   3. the body is alerted by T cells to produce these disease fighters

_____   4. kills microbes on living tissues

B_____   5. microbes found in 3 basic shapes—cocci, bacilli, and spirilla

_____   6. food poisoning caused by improperly canned food

C_____   7. uncontrolled growth of cells

_____   8. able to transfer the disease without showing symptoms of the disease

_____   9. government agency on the alert for outbreaks of disease

_____   10. treatment of cancer with chemicals

_____   11. contagious

D_____ 12. the "D" in the DPT shot

_____ 13. kills microbes on nonliving surfaces

E_____ 14. large numbers of people getting a disease in a short period of time

_____ 15. promoted use of chemicals to treat disease; he used salvarsan

F_____ 16. government agency that has to approve new drugs sold in the USA

_____ 17. received Nobel Prize for his discovery of penicillin

----

SECTION TWO

G_____ 18. common name given to microbes that cause disease

_____ 19. STD caused by a bacterium and treated with penicillin

H_____ 20. a disabling disease that attacks the liver

_____ 21. virus that causes AIDS

_____ 22. educated guess

I _____ 23. ability of the body to defend itself against disease without becoming sick

_____ 24. worldwide epidemic of 1918

J _____ 25. English doctor who developed the first successful vaccine; a nearby town is named in his honor

K_____ 26. he developed a set of steps to identify the microbe that causes a particular disease

L_____ 27. promoted the use of disinfectants: a mouthwash is named in his honor

_____ 28. we are all in danger of this disease caused by bacteria and transmitted through ticks

_____29. cells in body that produce our great antibodies

M_____30. the "MM" in MMR shots

_____31. microcopic organism

N_____32. immunity that you receive from your mother during her pregnancy

O_____33. a complete living thing

P _____34. made milk safer to drink; studied the disease rabies

----

SECTION THREE

_____35. microbe that causes disease

_____36. disease that attacks the nerves that control muscles

Q_____37. to isolate an ill person to try to stop the spread of a disease

R_____38. German measles

S _____ 39. became famous when he developed the first polio vaccine; tried to find a vaccine to work against AIDS

_____40. first disease to be eliminated due to a worldwide vaccination program

_____41. if we reduce this with a healthy lifestyle, we can improve our health

T_____42. master coordinators of our immune system

_____ 43. we receive a booster shot of this; the shot contains antibodies; get immunity from a DPT shot

U_____44. one way that AIDS is spread

V_____ 45. a shot that causes the body to develop antibodies against a disease

_____46. the study of viruses

W_____47. cells produced in bone marrow, the lymph system, and the spleen that fight disease

_____48. it's the common name for pertussis

X _____49. virus reproduction is like this; your copy of this review was made this way

Y _____50. almost done—YEAH!!

Z _____51. study of animals

Student Favorites

Amery, Heather, and Jane Songi. 1994. *Discover Hidden Worlds: The Home*. New York: Scholastic.

Buchman, Dian Dincin. 1992. *Medical Mysteries: Six Deadly Cases*. New York: Scholastic.

Churchill, E. Richard. 1989. *Optical Illusion Tricks and Toys*. New York: Sterling.

Clarke, Barry. 1990. *Eyewitness Juniors: Amazing Frogs and Toads*. New York: Alfred A. Knopf.

Cobb, Vicki. 1972. *Science Experiments You Can Eat*. New York: Harper & Row.

———. 1997. *Blood and Gore*. New York: Scholastic.

Curie, Eve. 1937. *Madame Curie*. Garden City: Doubleday, Doran.

Dewan, Ted. 1992. *Inside the Whale and Other Animals*. New York: Doubleday.

Greenberg, David. 1983. *Slugs*. Boston: Little, Brown.

Grillone, Lisa, and Joseph Gennaro. 1978. *Small Worlds Close Up*. New York: Crown.

Guinness Publishing Ltd. 1999. *The Guinness Book of World Records*. New York: Bantam.

Hellemans, Alexander, and Bryan Bunch. 1988. *The Timetables of Science: A Chronology of the Most Important People and Events in the History of Science*. New York: Simon & Schuster.

Herriot, James. 1972. *All Creatures Great and Small*. New York: St. Martin's.

Hersey, John. 1985. *Hiroshima*. New York: Vintage.

Langer, Richard W. 1969. *The After-Dinner Gardening Book*. New York: Collier.

Larson, Gary. 1980. *The Far Side Gallery*. Kansas City: Andrews, McNeel & Parker.

Lauber, Patricia. 1986. *Volcano: The Eruption and Healing of Mount St. Helens*. New York: Trumpet Club.

Macauley, David. 1988. *The Way Things Work*. Boston: Houghton Mifflin.

Nye, Bill. 1993. *Bill Nye, The Science Guy's Big Blast of Science*. Reading, MA: Addison-Wesley.

Reading's Fun, Ltd. 1994. *Warm and Fuzzy: The Most Adorable Animal Pictures Ever*. North Sydney, Australia: Weldon Russell.

Roberts, Royston M. 1989. *Serendipity: Accidental Discoveries in Science*. New York: John Wiley.

Schwartz, David M. 1985. *How Much Is a Million?* New York: Lothrop, Lee & Shepard.

Simon, Seymour. 1997. *Lightning*. New York: Scholastic.

Tomb, Howard, and Dennis Kunkel. 1993. *Microaliens: Dazzling Journeys with an Electron Microscope*. New York: Scholastic.

Treat, Lawrence. 1983. *You're the Detective*. New York: Trumpet Club.

Allen, Janet. 1995. *It's Never Too Late: Leading Adolescents to Lifelong Literacy.* Portsmouth, NH: Heinemann.

Allington, Richard. 1975. "Sustained Approaches to Reading and Writing." *Language Arts* 52 (6): 813–15.

Allison, Linda. 1976. *Blood and Guts: A Working Guide to Your Own Insides.* New York: Little, Brown.

American Society for Training and Development (ASTD). 2001. *What Employers Want.* Report of a survey conducted with the U.S. Department of Labor. www.arp.sprnet.org/admin/supt/want.htm.

Anderson, Richard C., Elfrieda H. Heibert, Janet A. Scott, and Ian A. G. Wilkinson. 1985. *Becoming a Nation of Readers*: *The Report of the Commission on Reading.* Washington, DC: National Institute of Education.

Anderson, Richard C., and P. David Pearson. 1978. *Teaching Reading Comprehension.* New York: Macmillan.

———. 1984. "A Schema-Theoretic View of Basic Processes in Reading." In *Handbook of Reading Research*, edited by P. D. Pearson et al. New York: Longman.

Anderson, Thomas H. 1980. "Study Strategies and Adjunct Aids." In *Theoretical Issues in Reading Comprehension*, edited by R. J. Spiro, B. C. Bruce, and W. F. Brewer, 483– 502. Hillsdale, NJ: Erlbaum.

Anderson, Thomas H., and Bonnie B. Armbruster. 1984. "Studying." In *Handbook of Reading Research*, edited by P. D. Pearson et al. New York: Longman.

Apple, Michael W. 1996. *Cultural Politics and Education.* New York: Teachers College Press.

Applebee, Arthur N. 1984. *Contexts for Learning to Write: Studies of Secondary School Instruction.* Norwood, NJ: Ablex.

Atwell, Nancie. 1987. *In the Middle: Writing, Reading, and Learning with Adolescents.* Portsmouth, NH: Heinemann Boynton/Cook.

———. 1998. *In the Middle: New Understandings About Writing, Reading, and Learning.* 2d ed. Portsmouth, NH: Heinemann Boynton/Cook.

Betts, Emmett. 1946. *Foundations of Reading Instruction.* New York: American Book.

Bimes-Michalak, Beverly. 1990. Writing Across the Curriculum. Presentation for Berks County, Intermediate Unit, Reading, Pennsylvania, 26 March.

Botel, Morton. 1977. *The Pennsylvania Comprehensive Reading/Communication Arts Plan (PCRP).* Harrisburg, PA: Pennsylvania Department of Education.

Britton, James, T. Burgess, Nancy Martin, A. McLeod, and H. Rosen. 1975. *The Development of Writing Abilities (11–18).* London: Macmillan.

Bruner, Jerome. 1986. *Actual Minds, Possible Worlds.* Cambridge, MA: Harvard University Press.

Buchman, Dian D. 1992. *Medical Mysteries: Six Deadly Cases.* New York: Scholastic.

Butler, Kathleen A. 1984. *Learning and Teaching Style: In Theory and Practice*. Columbia, CT: The Learner's Dimension.

Calinger, Ronald S. 1997. Archimedes. *World Book Encyclopedia*. Chicago: World Books, Inc., 604–605.

Calkins, Lucy M. 1986. *The Art of Teaching Writing*. Portsmouth, NH: Heinemann.

———. 1994. *The Art of Teaching Writing*. 2d ed. Portsmouth, NH: Heinemann.

Calkins, Lucy M., with Shelley Harwayne. 1991. *Living Between the Lines*. Portsmouth, NH: Heinemann.

Caverly, David C., and Vincent P. Orlando. 1991. "Textbook Study Strategies." In *Teaching Reading and Study Strategies at the College Level*, edited by D. C. Caverly and R. F. Flippo. Newark, DE: International Reading Association.

Church, Francis P. 1897. "Yes, Virginia, There Is a Santa Claus." *The New York Sun*, 21 September.

Clancy, Tom. 2000. *The Bear and the Dragon*. New York: Putnam.

Clay, Marie. 1967. "The Reading Behavior of Five-Year-Old Children: A Research Report." *New Zealand Journal of Education Studies*: 11–31.

———. 1991. *Becoming Literate: The Construction of Inner Control*. Portsmouth, NH: Heinemann.

Cochran-Smith, Marilyn, and Susan Lytle. 1993. *Inside/Outside: Teacher Research and Knowledge*. New York: Teachers College Press.

Cohn, Amy L., comp. 1993. *From Sea to Shining Sea: A Treasury of American Folklore and Folk Song*. New York: Scholastic.

Cohn, Melvin. 1994. "The Wisdom of Hindsight" in *Annual Review of Immunology*, vol. 12. Palo Alto, CA: Annual Reviews.

Coles, Gerald. 2000. *Misreading Reading. The Bad Science That Hurts Children*. Portsmouth, NH: Heinemann.

Dale, Edgar, and Jeanne Chall. 1948. "A Formula for Predicting Readability." *Educational Research Bulletin* 27: 11–20. Columbus: Ohio State University.

Dewey, John. 1916. *Democracy and Education*. New York: Free Press.

———. 1938. *Experience and Education*. New York: Free Press.

Dole, Janice A., Gerald Duffy, Laura R. Roehler, and P. David Pearson. 1991. "Moving from the Old to the New." *Review of Educational Research* 61: 239–64.

Downing, Charles R., and Owen L. Miller. 1990. *Cranial Creations: Forty-five Cooperative Learning Activities for Life Science Classes*. Portland, ME: J. Weston Walch.

Fader, Daniel N., and Elton B. McNeil. 1968. *Hooked on Books: Program and Proof*. New York: Berkley.

Faigley, Lester, and Stephen Witte. 1981. "Analyzing Revision." *College Composition* 32: 400–10.

Farr, Robert. 1996. Staff newsletter to faculty. Oxford, PA, 5 February.

Flesch, Rudolph. 1955. *Why Johnny Can't Read*. New York: Harper & Row.

Foreign Policy Association, ed. 1976. *A Cartoon History of United States Foreign Policy 1776–1976*. Washington, D.C.: Foreign Policy Association.

Freire, Paulo. 1985. *The Politics of Education: Culture, Power, and Liberation*. Hadley, MA: Bergin & Garvey.

———. 1989. *Education for Critical Consciousness*. New York: Continuum.

Fry, Edward. 1977. "Fry's Readability Graph: Clarifications, Validity, and Extension to Level 17." *Journal of Reading* 21: 242–52.

Fulwiler, Toby. 1987. *The Journal Book.* Portsmouth, NH: Heinemann.

Gardner, Howard. 1993. *Frames of Mind: The Theory of Multiple Intelligences.* New York: HarperCollins.

Gibboney, Richard A. 1994. *The Stone Trumpet.* Albany, NY: SUNY Press.

Gibboney, Richard A., and Clark D. Webb. 1998. *What Every Great Teacher Knows: Practical Principles for Effective Teaching.* Brandon, VT: Holistic Education.

Goodlad, John I. 1984. *A Place Called School: Prospects for the Future.* New York: McGraw-Hill.

Goodman, Kenneth. 1984. *Reading Strategies: Focus on Comprehension.* Katonah, NY: Richard C. Owen.

Graves, Donald H. 1978. "Balance the Basics: Let Them Write." New York: Ford Foundation.

———. 1983. *Writing: Teachers and Children at Work.* Portsmouth, NH: Heinemann.

———. 1991. *Build a Literate Classroom.* Portsmouth, NH: Heinemann.

Gregorc, Anthony. 1986. *Gregorc Style Delineator Developmental, Technical, and Administrative Manual.* Rev. ed. Columbia, CT: Gregorc Associates.

Guinness Publishing Ltd. 1999. *The Guinness Book of World Records.* New York: Bantam.

Hammond, W. Dorsey. 1985. Reading Comprehension Skills: Developing Them Across the Curriculum. Presentation for Learning Institute, Valley Forge, Pennsylvania, 11 December.

———. 1985. *Reading Comprehension Skills: Developing Them Across the Curriculum.* Springhouse, Pennsylvania: Springhouse Corporation.

Harste, Jerome, and Kathy Short, with Carolyn Burke. 1988. "Journal Writing." In *Creating Classrooms for Authors.* Portsmouth, NH: Heinemann.

Harwayne, Shelley. 1992. *Lasting Impressions: Weaving Literature into the Writing Workshop.* Portsmouth, NH: Heinemann.

Herber, Harold. 1970. *Reading in the Content Areas.* Englewood Cliffs, NJ: Prentice Hall.

Hersey, John. 1985. *Hiroshima.* Repr. ed. New York: Vintage.

Hillocks, George, Jr. 1987. "What Works in Teaching Composition: A Meta-analysis of Experimental Treatment Studies." *American Journal of Education* 93: 133–70.

Hoffman, Sandra Josephs, and Donna Hooker Topping. 1999. "Changing the Face of Teaching and Learning Through Teacher Research." In *Creative Teaching: Act 2*, edited by Hans Klein. Madison, WI: Omni.

Holdaway, Don. 1979. *The Foundations of Literacy.* Portsmouth, NH: Heinemann.

Hunt, Lyman. 1967. "Evaluation Through Teacher-Pupil Conferences." In *The Evaluation of Children's Reading Achievement*, edited by T. C. Barrett, 111–26. Newark, DE: International Reading Association.

Hunter, Madeline. 1984. "Knowing, Teaching, and Supervising." In *Using What We Know About Teaching*, edited by P. L. Hosford. Alexandria, VA: Association for Supervision and Curriculum Development.

"Idea Exchange." 1992. *NEA Today* (May): 10.

Jackson, Alan Eugene, and Randy Bruce Traywick. *From a Distance.* Julie Gold. Los Angeles: WB Music Corporation. ASCAP Title Code 360291543.

Jehlen, Alain. 2000. "Science Texts Flunk." *NEA Today* (April): 29.

Jensen, Eric. 1998. *Teaching with the Brain in Mind.* Alexandria, VA: Association for Supervision and Curriculum Development.

Joyce, Bruce, and Marsha Weil. 1986. *Models of Teaching,* 3d ed. Englewood Cliffs, NJ: Prentice Hall.

Kadaba, L. S. 2001. "A Teacher's Infectious Tunes." *Philadelphia Inquirer,* 2 May, D1–D3.

Kagan, Spencer. 1988. *Cooperative Learning.* San Juan Capistrano, CA: Resources for Teachers.

Kiester, E., Jr. 1990. "A Curiosity Turned into the First Silver Bullet Against Death." *Smithsonian* Vol. 21: No. 8 (November): 173–87.

Kirby, Dan. 1981. "The J." In *Inside Out: Developmental Strategies for Teaching Writing.* Edited by Dan Kirby and Tom Liner. Portsmouth, NH: Heinemann.

Kohn, Alfie. 2000. *The Case Against Standardized Testing: Raising the Scores, Ruining the Schools.* Portsmouth, NH: Heinemann.

Krashen, Stephen. 1999. *Three Arguments Against Whole Language and Why They Are Wrong.* Portsmouth, NH: Heinemann.

Langer, Richard W. 1969. *The After-Dinner Gardening Book.* New York: Collier.

Lavin, Christine. *The Amoeba Hop.* Englewood, NJ: PKM Music. ASCAP Title Code 310227242.

Lytle, Susan, and Morton Botel. 1988. *Pennsylvania Framework for Reading, Writing, and Talking Across the Curriculum.* Harrisburg, PA: Pennsylvania Department of Education.

McCarrier, Andrea, Gay Su Pinnell, and Irene C. Fountas. 2000. *Interactive Writing: How Language and Literacy Come Together, K–2.* Portsmouth, NH: Heinemann.

McCarthy, Bernice. 2000. *About Learning,* rev. ed. New York: Excel.

McCracken, Robert, and Marlene McCracken. 1972. *Reading Is Only the Tiger's Tail.* San Rafael, CA: Leswing.

McKeown, Margaret, Isabel Beck and Rebecca Hamilton. 1997. *Questioning the Author: An Approach for Enhancing Student Engagement With Text.* Newark, DE: International Reading Association.

Michaels, Ski. 1992. *102 Creepy, Crawly Bug Jokes.* N.p.: Watermill Press.

Murray, Donald M. 1989. *Expecting the Unexpected: Teaching Myself—and Others—to Read and Write.* Portsmouth, NH: Heinemann.

Muther, Connie. 1985. "What Every Textbook Evaluator Should Know." *Educational Leadership* 42 (7): 4–8.

National Association of Colleges and Employers. 2000. "Ideal Candidate Has Top-Notch Interpersonal Skills, Say Employers." *NACE Press Room,* 18 January. Available from http://www.naceweb.org/press/display.cfm/2000/pr011800.htm.

North, Stephen M. 1987. *The Making of Knowledge in Composition: Portrait of an Emerging Field.* Portsmouth, NH: Heinemann.

Ogle, Donna M. 1986. "K-W-L: A Teaching Model That Develops Active Reading of Expository Text." *The Reading Teacher* 39: 564–70.

Optiz, Michael F., and Timothy V. Rasinski. 1998. *Good-Bye Round Robin: Twenty-Five Effective Oral Reading Strategies.* Portsmouth, NH: Heinemann.

Palinscar, Annmarie, and Ann L. Brown. 1984. "Reciprocal Teaching of Comprehension-Fostering and Monitoring Strategies." *Cognition and Instruction* 1: 117–75.

Panati, Charles. 1987. *Panati's Extraordinary Origins of Everyday Things.* New York: Harper and Row.

Paris, Scott G., Marjorie Lipson, and Karen Wixson. 1993. "Becoming a Strategic Reader." *Contemporary Educational Psychology* 8: 293–316.

Pearson, P. David, and Linda G. Fielding. 1991. "Comprehension Instruction." In *Handbook of Reading Research*, vol. 2, edited by R. Barr, M. L. Kamil, P. B. Mosenthal, and P. D. Pearson. New York: Longman.

Pearson, P. David, and Dale Johnson. 1978. *Teaching Reading Comprehension.* New York: Holt, Rinehart & Winston.

Pilgreen, Janice. 2000. *The SSR Handbook: How to Organize and Manage a Sustained Silent Reading Program.* Portsmouth, NH: Heinemann.

Play Ball! 1998. Cleveland, Ohio: TELARC CD-80468.

Postman, Neil. 1985. *Amusing Ourselves to Death.* New York: Viking.

Ravitch, Diane. 1983. "The Education Pendulum." *Psychology Today* (October): 62–71.

Roberts, Royston M. 1989. *Serendipity: Accidental Discoveries in Science.* New York: John Wiley.

Robinson, Frank. 1961. *Effective Study.* New York: Harper & Row.

Rockapella. 1992. "Capital." From *Where in the World is Carmen San Diego?* New York: Zoom Express.

Routman, Regie. 1996. *Literacy at the Crossroads: Crucial Talk About Reading, Writing, and Other Teaching Dilemmas.* Portsmouth, NH: Heinemann.

———. 2000. *Conversations.* Portsmouth, NH: Heinemann.

Rowe, Mary Budd. 1974. "Wait-Time and Rewards as Instructional Variables, Their Influence on Language, Logic, and Fate Control: Part One, Wait-Time." *Journal of Research in Science Teaching* 2: 81–94.

Santa, Carol M. 1988. *Content Reading Including Study Systems: Reading, Writing, and Studying Across the Curriculum.* Dubuque, IA: Kendall/Hunt.

Smith, Frank. 1986. *Understanding Reading.* Hillsdale, NJ: Erlbaum.

———. 1988. *Joining the Literacy Club: Further Essays Into Education.* Portsmouth, NH: Heinemann.

Spache, George. 1953. "A New Readability Formula for Primary-Grade Reading Materials." *Elementary School Journal* 53: 410–13.

Stauffer, Russell. 1975. *Directing the Reading-Thinking Process.* New York: Harper & Row.

Taylor, Denny. 1998. *Beginning to Read and the Spin Doctors of Science.* Urbana, IL: National Council of Teachers of English.

Teale, William, and Elizabeth Sulzby. 1989. "Emerging Literacy: New Perspectives." In *Emerging Literacy: Young Children Learn to Read and Write*, edited by D. S. Strickland and L. M. Morrow. Newark, DE: International Reading Association.

Temple, Clivia, and Robert K. G. Temple, trans. 1998. *Aesop: The Complete Fables.* New York: Penguin Classics.

Tierney, Robert. 1984. "Writing to Learn." Department of the Month: Language Arts. *Curriculum Product Review*, April.

Tompkins, Gail E. 2001. *Language Arts: Content and Teaching Strategies.* 5th ed. Upper Saddle River, NJ: Prentice Hall.

Topping, Donna Hooker. n.d. "We Don't Hear Many Teacher Voices. Why?" [Working title.] Manuscript in progress.

Topping, Donna Hooker, and Sandra Josephs Hoffman. Forthcoming 2002. "Helping Teachers Become Teacher-Researchers." *Journal of Reading Education*.

Topping, Donna Hooker, and Roberta Ann McManus. 1993. "Listening to Students Talking About How We Teach." Manuscript.

Trelease, Jim. 1989. *The New Read-Aloud Handbook*. New York: Penguin.

———. 1995. *The Read-Aloud Handbook*. 4th ed. New York: Penguin.

Tsujimoto, Joseph. 2001. *Lighting Fires: How the Passionate Teacher Engages Adolescent Writers*. Portsmouth, NH: Heinemann.

Tyack, David, and Larry Cuban. 1995. *Tinkering Toward Utopia: A Century of Public School Reform*. Cambridge, MA: Harvard University Press.

Vacca, Richard T., and JoAnne L. Vacca. 1996. *Content Area Reading*. 5th Ed. New York: HarperCollins.

Vygotsky, Lev S. 1962. *Mind and Society: The Development of Higher Psychological Processes*. Cambridge, MA: MIT Press.

———. 1978. *Thought and Language*. Cambridge MA: MIT Press.

"Wakko's America." 1983. *Stephen Spielberg Presents ANIMANIACS*. Burbank, CA: Warner.

Weehawken, NJ Public Schools. 1974. *Individualized Language Arts: Diagnosis, Prescription, Evaluation*. A Teachers' Resource Manual for the Promotion of Students' Facility in Written Composition, Grades K–12. Weehawken, NJ: Board of Education.

Welsh, Patrick. 1986. *Tales Out of School*. New York: Penguin.

Winn, Marie. 1985. *The Plug-in Drug*. New York: Penguin.

———. 1987. *Unplugging the Plug-in Drug*. New York: Penguin.

Wiscont, Jeanne Mull. 1990. "A Study of the Sustained Silent Reading Program for Intermediate Grade Students in the Pulaski, Wisconsin, School District." Master's thesis, University of Wisconsin. ERIC, ED 323520.

Wood, Karen D., Diane Lapp, and James Flood. 1992. *Guiding Readers Through Texts: A Review of Study Guides*. Newark, DE: International Reading Association.